Transcribing Talk and Interaction

Transcribing Talk and Interaction

Issues in the representation of communication data

Christopher Joseph Jenks
City University Hong Kong

John Benjamins Publishing Company
Amsterdam / Philadelphia

The paper used in this publication meets the minimum requirements of American National Standard for Information Sciences – Permanence of Paper for Printed Library Materials, ANSI z39.48-1984.

Library of Congress Cataloging-in-Publication Data

Jenks, Christopher Joseph.
 Transcribing talk and interaction : issues in the representation of communication data / Christopher Joseph Jenks.
     p. cm.
Includes bibliographical references and index.
1. Oral Communication--Research. 2. Discourse analysis--Research.
P95.3.J46   2011
302.2'242--dc23   2011018542
ISBN 978 90 272 1183 5 (HB; alk. paper) / ISBN 978 90 272 1184 2 (PB; alk. paper)
ISBN 978 90 272 8506 5 (EB)

© 2011 – John Benjamins B.V.
No part of this book may be reproduced in any form, by print, photoprint, microfilm, or any other means, without written permission from the publisher.

John Benjamins Publishing Co. · P.O. Box 36224 · 1020 ME Amsterdam · The Netherlands
John Benjamins North America · P.O. Box 27519 · Philadelphia PA 19118-0519 · USA

Table of contents

Preface: An introduction to this book — IX

CHAPTER 1
An introduction to transcripts of talk and interaction — 1
1.1 Introduction   1
1.2 What are transcripts of talk and interaction?   2
1.3 What are transcripts used for?   5
1.4 What are the benefits of using transcripts?   7
1.5 Are transcripts accurate representations of talk and interaction?   9

CHAPTER 2
Theoretical issues — 11
2.1 Introduction   11
2.2 Transcript as research construct   11
2.3 Transcript variation   14
2.4 Transcription politics   18
2.5 Transcription ethics   21

CHAPTER 3
Transcribing talk and interaction: The basics — 25
3.1 Introduction   25
3.2 Playback   26
   3.2.1 Software issues   27
   3.2.2 Hardware issues   28
3.3 Organization   29
   3.3.1 Layout   29
   3.3.2 Line numbers   34
   3.3.3 Line breaks   35
   3.3.4 Spacing   37
   3.3.5 Placement of transcript   39

3.4 Content 39
    3.4.1 Font type 39
    3.4.2 Speaker representation 41
    3.4.3 Transcription detail 42

CHAPTER 4
Transcribing interactional and paralinguistic features   45
4.1 Introduction 45
4.2 Transcription conventions 46
4.3 Interactional features 48
    4.3.1 Turn-taking 48
        4.3.1.1 Simultaneous utterances 48
        4.3.1.2 Overlapping utterances 49
        4.3.1.3 Contiguous utterances 51
    4.3.2 Pauses 52
        4.3.2.1 Timed pauses 53
        4.3.2.2 Micro pauses 53
4.4 Paralinguistic features 54
    4.4.1 Intonation 55
        4.4.1.1 Falling intonation 56
        4.4.1.2 Slight rising intonation 56
        4.4.1.3 Rising intonation 57
        4.4.1.4 Marked upsteps/downsteps in intonation 57
    4.4.2 Elongations and abrupt stops 59
        4.4.2.1 Elongations 59
        4.4.2.2 Abrupt stops 60
    4.4.3 Stress and voice amplitude 60
        4.4.3.1 Emphasis 60
        4.4.3.2 Loud/forte speech 61
        4.4.3.3 Soft/piano speech 62
    4.4.4 Audible aspirations and inhalations 63
        4.4.4.1 Exhalations 63
        4.4.4.2 Laugh particle 64
        4.4.4.3 Laughter within an utterance 64
        4.4.4.4 Inhalations 65
    4.4.5 Tempo 66
        4.4.5.1 Faster/allegro talk 66
        4.4.5.2 Slower/lento talk 66

    4.4.6 Other voice qualities   67
        4.4.6.1 Smile voice   67
    4.4.7 Unintelligible speech   68
        4.4.7.1 Unintelligible syllable   68
        4.4.7.2 Hearing approximations   69

CHAPTER 5
Transcribing nonverbal conduct　　　　　　　　　　　　　　　　　71
5.1 Introduction   71
5.2 Nonverbal conduct   73
    5.2.1 Body postures   75
    5.2.2 Facial expressions   75
    5.2.3 Gestures   75
    5.2.4 Gaze   76
    5.2.5 Proximity   77
    5.2.6 Actions   77
5.3 Media used to represent nonverbal behavior   78
    5.3.1 Text   79
    5.3.2 Video stills   80
    5.3.3 Drawings   82
    5.3.4 Digital renderings   83
5.4 Methods for representing sequentiality   84
    5.4.1 Symbols   85
    5.4.2 Sequencing   86
    5.4.3 Time stamps   87

CHAPTER 6
Advanced issues　　　　　　　　　　　　　　　　　　　　　　　89
6.1 Introduction   89
6.2 Advanced theoretical issues   89
    6.2.1 Myopia   90
        6.2.1.1 Tunnel vision   91
        6.2.1.2 Emotional attachment   92
    6.2.2 Present and recall   93
    6.2.3 Outsourcing   94
6.3 Advanced practical issues   95
    6.3.1 Capitalization   96
    6.3.2 Apostrophes   97

      6.3.3 Conversational floors   98
      6.3.4 Translations   99
      6.3.5 Add-on conventions   100
      6.3.6 Transcription software   100
6.4 Conclusion   103

References   105

Appendices   109
    Appendix A   109
    Example transcript

    Appendix B   114
    Transcription conventions

    Appendix C   115
    Transcription conventions comparison table

    Appendix D   116
    Quick start guide to transcribing

Index   119

Preface
An introduction to this book

This book has been written because I believe researchers and postgraduate students who are beginning to explore the world of spoken discourse analysis have few publications to choose from that comprehensively review the theoretical and practical issues of transcribing communication data. A quick scan of the literature reveals that very few transcription books have been published in the past three decades. This is an astonishing fact given that there are perhaps hundreds of books published on spoken discourse analysis. This imbalance comes at a time when more and more researchers are using some form of spoken discourse analysis to conduct research. A second, but equally important reason for writing this book is my belief that transcribing is a skill – as is analyzing data recordings – that should not be taken for granted. Transcribing is a skill that is especially important in the human and social sciences, as a very large body of research – both qualitative and quantitative – draws on transcripts of talk and interaction. The third and final reason for writing this book stems from my experience teaching transcribing to university students. Nearly all of my students over the years begin my courses with virtually no experience in transcribing data recordings. Despite a growing body of literature related to transcription issues, most existing publications do not address the needs of these students because they are written for audiences with advanced and specialized knowledge. To a large extent, the content of this book has been put together with these students in mind. I hope that this book introduces the necessary topics to develop the skill of transcribing for these students, while promoting the need to problematize the role transcripts play in conducting research.

There are six chapters in this book. Chapter 1 provides a general introduction to transcripts. The chapter, for example, defines transcripts of talk and interaction, and identifies reasons for using transcripts to conduct research. Chapter 2 identifies the many overlooked, but important theoretical issues that underpin the task of transcribing communication data. For example, how much detail should be included in a transcript, and what are theoretical reasons that underpin the decision to determine levels of detail? Are there any ethical issues that must be taken into consideration whilst transcribing communication data? What impact do transcripts have in the lives of those recorded, and for those researchers who have access to research participants?

Chapter 3 discusses the fundamentals of transcribing communication data. The chapter begins by identifying hardware and software issues that transcribers must address while transcribing communication data. The focus then shifts to a more general discussion of transcript organization and data representation. Here the reader is given a comprehensive and detailed overview of the different ways in which the verbal and nonverbal aspects of communication can be represented in transcript form, and why each organizational issue is important to the representation of communication data. Chapter 4 provides an overview of how to transcribe interactional and paralinguistic features. The chapter is divided into two sections: interactional and paralinguistic features. Example transcripts are provided in each section, and advice given throughout the chapter. Each section can be read in sequence, or independently as in a reference book.

Chapter 5 presents approaches to transcribing nonverbal conduct. The chapter discusses the dynamic nature of nonverbal conduct, and reviews several methods used to transcribe body positions and movements. Chapter 6 reviews advanced transcription issues. For example, how does a transcriber's level of involvement in the transcription process shape what appears in a transcript? Is it good transcription practice to be responsible for all aspects of transcribing, or can transcribers outsource their transcription work?

The contents of this book represent many years of teaching transcript-based research to postgraduate students, as well as my interest in, and application of, conversation analysis and interactional sociolinguistics. I have tried to write this book in clear and simple English, while being faithful to the complexities of transcribing communication data. Although the chapters in this book cover a broad spectrum of transcription issues, becoming a good transcriber requires many years of practice listening to, watching, and then transcribing communication data. Transcribing is largely a hands-on process that requires the ability to decipher between a marked upstep and rise in intonation, select the most appropriate visual medium for representing an arm extension, and accurately capture the particularities of a regional accent, to name a few. Hopefully this book will encourage other academics responsible for the teaching of transcript-based research to create multimedia activities in their courses aimed at promoting the development of these skills. With this in mind, this book should be read while doing some form of transcript-based research and/or used in conjunction with a course on spoken discourse analysis (e.g., conversation analysis, discourse analysis, discursive psychology, and critical discourse analysis). Chapters can be read in order, or used as points of reference for specific theoretical and/or practical transcription issues.

Finally, I wish to thank my colleagues and friends for their thoughtful advice and professional support, especially Adam Brandt, Spencer Hazel, Kristian Mortensen, Andrew Harris, and Olcay Sert. I am likewise indebted to the many students that have taken my course and forced me to answer difficult questions. Special thanks must also be given to the editors and reviewers of John Benjamins; their expertise and advice provided much help on earlier versions of the manuscript. Last, but not least, I would like to thank my wife, Jin, for her emotional support and encouragement. This book would not have been possible without her.

CHAPTER 1

An introduction to transcripts of talk and interaction

1.1 Introduction

Our communicative encounters with people are often so mundane and instinctive that we forget how multifaceted the phenomenon is.

In a busy cafe, ordering a cup of coffee may require the use of gestures, in addition to the spoken language, all while simultaneously managing a conversation with a work colleague. A family dinner may entail conversing with multiple interactants on multiple topics, where fluctuation in voice amplitude and the use of gaze play an important role in how turns are managed. While participation in communication is done with ostensible ease, transcribing these multifaceted communicative acts require extensive knowledge and practice.

This book provides a comprehensive account of current introductory issues in transcribing talk and interaction. The book is intended for postgraduate students and researchers making the transition into transcript-based research. This particular audience often possesses a desire – or need, in the case of postgraduate students – to use discourse/conversation analysis or similar analytic methods of investigation (e.g., interactional sociolinguistics) to examine issues and themes related to communication, particularly in its spoken form, but have little to no knowledge of good transcription practice. Readers who are studying and/or working in sociology, education, anthropology, psychology, or linguistics, will find this book particularly helpful in that these disciplines have long-standing traditions in using transcripts to investigate talk and interaction.

Despite a plethora of textbooks and monographs that discuss approaches to analyzing talk and interaction – from introductory books on conversation analysis to specific book-length studies on discourse markers – there are substantially fewer books devoted to the theoretical, methodological, and practical issues of transcribing communication data. What is the 'best' system to represent, in transcripts, the intricate ways in which people use voice and gesture? Are there any political and ethical implications in transcribing a particular speech community? What font type and size should be used whilst transcribing? These are the types of questions that will be answered in this book.

2 Transcribing talk and interaction

Before addressing these specific transcription issues, this chapter will define transcripts of talk and interaction, and identify what they are used for. The chapter then identifies the benefits of using detailed transcripts to investigate the ways in which people talk and interact. This discussion is followed by an exploration of what transcription accuracy means in the representation of talk and interaction.

1.2 What are transcripts of talk and interaction?

The Oxford Dictionary of English (Soanes & Stevenson, 2005, p. 1872) defines a transcript as "a written or printed version of material originally presented in another medium." In the case of communication data, the 'medium' in which transcripts are based are the observations and data recordings of social-interactional events (e.g., teaching a lesson or having a conversation at a restaurant). Transcripts are sometimes produced *in situ*, as the social-interactional event unfolds. Stenographers, for example, are commonly employed to produce real-time transcripts during courtroom talk or for closed captioning during televised news broadcasts. However, in most research for the human and social sciences, transcripts are created from video and/or audio recordings of events that have taken place in the past. The 'written or printed version' of data recordings includes text and/or visual material (e.g., pictures and drawings). The text material may minimally include a short narrative of a communicative event, as in Extract 1.

```
(1)   A tourist has just reached a merchant's store
      in a busy market. The merchant asks the
      tourist whether he would like something.
      The tourist responds by stating that he will
      enter the store and have a look.
```

While narratives allow researchers to describe a communicative event in great detail, they are often used to provide contextual information before the transcript is presented. Alternatively, the written version of the data recording could include a line-by-line account of what was actually said, as illustrated in Extract 2 (see Appendix A for the full version of the example transcript).

```
(2)   5   Merchant:   hello sir do you wanna
      6               something
      8   Peter:      walk in here and have a look
```

In addition to documenting what was said, line-by-line representations often include how words and utterances are said, as in Extract 3.

```
(3)   5   Merchant:   hello sir. (0.5) do↓ you↑
      6               wa↓nna↑ something?
```

```
    7                   (0.4)
    8   Peter:          walk in here and have a look.
```

In Extract 3, the punctuation markers (i.e., period/full stop and question mark) and symbols (i.e., arrows) represent intonation, while the numbers between parentheses denote pauses between spates of talk. The 'what' and the 'how' of talk and interaction provide analytically important information regarding the way interactants co-construct meaning (for an overview of different transcription conventions, see Chapter 4).

If the communicative event was recorded using a camcorder, then a video still is often used within the document, as shown in Extract 4.

```
(4)  A tourist has just reached a merchant's store
     in a busy market. The merchant asks the
     tourist whether he would like something.
     The tourist responds by stating that he will
     enter the store and have a look.
```

```
    5   Merchant:       hello sir. (0.5) do↓ you↑
    6                   wa↓nna↑ something?
    7                   (0.4)
    8   Peter:          walk in here and have a look.
```

Therefore, a transcript may include a short narrative, a line-by-line account of the talk and interaction, a video still (or drawing), or any combination of the three. Each type of representation encompasses varying degrees of detail (see Section 3.4.3). More importantly, the decision to select a particular type of representation is underpinned by different theoretical and methodological beliefs. As detailed later in Chapter 2, research traditions and investigatory aims lead to selective transcribing. The methodological framework adopted to analyze data recordings (i.e., conduct research) will often determine what to transcribe, and how to transcribe it (Ochs, 1979). Accordingly, it could be said that there is no universally supported way of transcribing communication data. As a result, there will always be variation in what is meant by transcripts of talk and interaction (see Duranti 2006, p. 301, for a concise overview of the evolution of transcripts in the humanities and social and behavioral sciences). For instance, transcripts sometimes include video clips if created and published in an electronic medium, the International Phonetic Alphabet is often incorporated to provide precise phonetic representation, and even musical notations are used to represent the rhythm of communication. Indeed, the very data recordings that are used to create transcripts are selective – and therefore transformational – in that the placement and quality of recording devices shape how much 'data' is captured, and thus transcribed (see Section 3.4.3). For instance, placing a video camera in the back of a classroom will capture what a teacher is doing and saying, but will miss out on most of the students' facial expressions and gaze. Furthermore, recording devices cannot fully capture all of the linguistic and interactional nuances of communication, as experienced *in situ* by the interactants under investigation.

While it is ultimately a researcher's decision to select one or more forms of representation, it is important to reemphasize the fact that transcripts are merely second-hand interpretations of communicative events. This is because transcripts are temporally and contextually displaced from the moment-by-moment unfolding of communication, as it occurs and is dealt with by the interactants under investigation. The issue of temporal and contextual displacement is most evident when researchers replay and dissect data recordings. In real-life social-interactional encounters, communication unfolds in a sequentially manner. Interactants do not have the opportunity to stop and rewind their ongoing talk, nor can they break up their interaction into smaller, more manageable parts. Therefore, transcripts are potentially misleading in that they can be disassembled into smaller stretches of talk, and presented according to particular empirical needs and wants. Transcripts are also inherently partial in that they are confined to the space available on a sheet of paper, and 'completed' with finite time and resources. In theory, however, transcripts are never complete, and in practice, constantly evolving, as subsequent readings will almost always result in slight modifications. That is to say, transcripts are not products, but rather a constantly evolving interpretive (cultural) process. The upshot is that transcripts "are not transparent and unproblematic records of scientific research..." (Bucholtz, 2000, p. 1440), and should always be used in conjunction with data recordings and any other supplementary data and resources available (e.g., field notes, documents, testimonies, feedback from a work colleague, speech analysis programs).

1.3 What are transcripts used for?

If transcripts are merely supplementary materials, and secondary to actual data recordings, then what purpose do they serve? Despite being inherently biased and selective, transcripts play an important role in conducting research. The four most fundamental transcription functions are to (1) represent, (2) assist, (3) disseminate, and (4) verify. First, transcripts are used to represent communicative events that have occurred in the past. Transcripts are created after communicative events have taken place because communication is not a fixed, spatial object that can be analyzed with great scrutiny in real time. In a similar vein, transcripts function as representations of talk and interaction in that they are created in a medium that is different than the communicative event. That is to say, transcripts are largely text-based documents that represent communication in a fixed state, whereas most communicative encounters are organically and dynamically produced (Bucholtz, 2007). It should be noted that audio and video recordings are also representations of communication in that they 'capture' events from strategically designated, sometimes biased areas. Despite the importance of data recordings, transcripts are (erroneously) considered the primary form of representation, as creating them requires a significant amount of interpretative work. Yet, in order to make empirically valid observations, transcripts and data recordings must be used simultaneously. Data recordings are necessary, as they allow instant and nearly unadulterated access through the lens of a camera (and/or audio microphone), while transcripts represent details of talk and interaction that are often overlooked by the naked eye (and/or ear).

This leads to the second transcription function: to assist. Whether working individually as a student on a dissertation or on a government-funded project with a group of researchers, transcripts are used to assist in the analysis of data. Data can come in the form of documents, interviews, and computer-generated speech analyses, to name a few, and transcripts should be used with any and all documents and resources available. Consider, for example, a hypothetical situation where a researcher is making empirical observations based on a video recording and transcript. Although the researcher will want to base her analyses on the actual data recordings, they are notoriously difficult to follow without a transcript (see Section 1.4). Transcripts are particularly helpful in conducting research in that they provide a level of detail that is nearly impossible to account for whilst listening and/or watching a recording of communication in real time. For example, a subtle shift in gaze or an onset of overlapping laughter occurs in a matter of milliseconds. Most researchers would find it impossible to sufficiently discuss such interactional phenomena without a corresponding transcript. Conversely, analyses based solely on transcripts will likely fail to capture the tenor and mood of the interactants and interaction. Therefore, transcripts play an important role in assisting in the analytic process, especially for the third transcription function: to disseminate.

That is, transcripts are used to disseminate observations and findings. Dissemination occurs at several stages of conducting research (Edwards & Lampert, 1993). During the early stages of analyzing data recordings, researchers typically share their preliminary transcripts and observations with their supervisory team, work colleagues, or peers within their respective disciplines. However, if researchers are working with confidential and sensitive data, then care must be taken to maintain anonymity while sharing their transcripts and observations. Sharing confidential and sensitive data requires researchers to mask the identities of the interactants under investigation (for a discussion of ethical issues related to transcribing communication data, see Chapter 2). Whether sharing data at a conference or with a small group of work colleagues, researchers will want to use their transcripts to test theories, share observations, and seek guidance regarding difficult-to-transcribe stretches of communication (see Section 3.2). Again, transcripts are constantly evolving, and there is no single way of transcribing a stretch of communication. An extra set of eyes will prove useful during the entire transcription process. The feedback received during this preliminary stage will often be used to refine (and re-refine) transcripts and observations until they are ready to be published or taken to an open domain (e.g., a university library, a course website, or an academic journal). Because the validity of the observations made and the quality of the research produced are dependent on the transcript, pre-publication dissemination is an important part of doing transcript-based research. Researchers often spend a significant part of their research time sharing their pre-published transcripts at workshops, conferences, and informal data sessions.

Finally, transcripts are used so that the academic community can verify the validity of the claims and observations made in an empirical study. In transcript-based research, the validity of a claim or observation is determined by examining the transcript from which the claim or observation has been made. The academic community will need and want to know whether any given claim or observation made is demonstrably relevant to the interactants and interaction represented in the transcript. Verification, of course, does not imply that everyone within the academic community will agree with the claims and observations made in an empirical study. Universal agreement within the academic community rarely occurs, and as a result, verification can often open transcripts, as well as claims and observations, to criticisms. This is a normal and healthy part of doing transcript-based research, especially if the criticisms are constructive.

1.4 What are the benefits of using transcripts?

As discussed in the beginning of this chapter, communication is a multifaceted phenomenon. Communication involves pauses that are carefully timed in order to project speakership, prosody that is strategically used to perform social actions, and gestures that are intertwined with speech in order to convey meaning, to name a few. Although the multifaceted nature of communication is difficult to monitor *in situ*, talk and interaction can be documented for later inspection. Perhaps the most common way of documenting communication is to create transcripts based on data recordings. Transcripts are invaluable empirical tools in that they document the intricate and minute details of communication, as it occurs and unfolds at the site of talk and interaction. The benefit more specifically – in terms of making analytic observations – lies in the fact that transcripts (and corresponding data recordings) can be analyzed over and over again while simultaneously dissecting talk and interaction into analytically manageable parts. The issue of dissecting transcripts into smaller, more manageable parts leads to the second benefit of using transcripts for communication research.

It is nearly impossible to analyze, and can indeed prove challenging to follow, an entire transcript based on a 5-minute data recording (see Appendix A, for example). The recording-to-page ratio for a transcript that is orthographically transcribed with only some prosodic information is approximately 1:2. That is, for each minute of recording, there will be approximately two pages of transcript. Therefore, a 5-minute recording will result in approximately ten pages of transcript. In order to make analytic observations that are presentable and/or publishable for an academic audience, the 10-page transcript must be broken down into smaller, more manageable parts/extracts. The medium and layout of a transcript allows for this type of dissection (for a discussion of layout and organization issues, see Chapter 3). For instance, Extract 3 above is reproduced below as Extract 5, as it represents three seconds of a larger 5-minute recording.

```
(5)  5   Merchant:   hello sir. (0.5) do↓ you↑
     6               wa↓nna↑ something?
     7               (0.4)
     8   Peter:      walk in here and have a look.
```

This smaller segment of talk is conducive to situating transcripts within larger analytic discussions. Imagine, for instance, the space and text required in making detailed observations on several minutes or more of continuous talk and interaction. The reader would be required to go back and forth numerous times, from transcript to observation, and from one page to another, potentially leading to reader confusion and frustration. In addition to assisting the reader, dissecting larger transcripts into smaller, more analytically manageable extracts provides more flexibility in how observations are organized. For instance, smaller segments can be presented sequentially in order to represent the overall flow and progression of communication, as in Extract 6, where three smaller extracts represent a larger opening exchange between a merchant and customer. Written analytic observations would typically follow each smaller extract, providing a more reader-friendly presentation of findings.

```
(6)  a.  1                    (7.2)
         2   Peter:            there it is, it's this way
         3                     ((inaudible))
     b.  4                     (10.9) ((walking to merchant))
         5   Merchant:         hello sir. (0.5) do↓ you↑
         6                     wa↓nna↑ something?
     c.  7                     (0.4)
         8   Peter:            walk in here and have a look.
```

Alternatively, separate segments can be organized as a collection of features in order to highlighted a common theme or pattern, as in Extract 7, where three extracts all represent instances when the customer asks the merchant a question. In this case, the written analytic observations would typically follow the last extract, and the observations would focus on the three extracts as a collection.

```
(7)  a.  65   Peter:      °(okay)° can- can↓ we↑ get one
         66                [so it's not like] that?
         67   Merchant:    [oh >okay. okay.>]
     b.  88   Peter:       [[so what's your price]]
         89   Merchant:    [[i'll give you a good]] price
     c.  101  Peter:       you su[re?
         102  Merchant:          [it was twenty (.) sure
         103                one hundred percent sure
```

Transcripts are also beneficial in that basic software programs have computer-assisted tools that quickly and accurately search for specific features of talk and interaction. Search tools are especially helpful when dealing with large corpora of data. For example, pressing 'CTRL or COMMAND + F' in most word processing programs will bring up a tool that will search through hundreds of pages of transcript within seconds, while concordance programs will conduct more advanced searches and compile analytic reports with little difficulty (see Adolphs, 2008). Moreover, transcription and observational comments and notes can easily be added to transcripts by using the many features available in word processing programs. Comments and notes can be used for anything from adding a reminder to transcribe something in more detail to making analytic notes for others to see

(see Section 3.3.3). In the same vein, during the dissemination stages of research, transcripts provide an excellent paper-based medium for making handwritten comments and providing feedback.

1.5 Are transcripts accurate representations of talk and interaction?

In conducting research on how people talk and interact, a common concern is whether the produced transcript accurately reflects the communication data. The issue of accuracy is important in transcript-based research, as misrepresentations of talk and interaction will lead to incorrect analytic observations. Furthermore, because at present most transcript-based research is published without easy access to the primary source of data, researchers have a professional commitment to ensuring that their transcripts accurately represent data recordings. Ensuring transcripts are accurate representations of talk and interaction is particularly important because it is common practice for one researcher to reference – and sometimes modify – transcripts published by another researcher (Bucholtz, 2007).

With the understanding that transcripts will never fully capture communication as it unfolds in real time, what then is an accurate representation of talk and interaction? Accurately representing talk and interaction does not necessarily require transcribing everything heard and seen in a data recording. That is, the issue of accuracy is not entirely dependent on detail. While detail generally positively correlates with accuracy, most researchers do not have the time and resources to produce transcripts that include every minute detail of talk and interaction. Thus, the need to capture as closely as possible what has been said and done in a data recording must be counterbalanced with the realities and practicalities of doing research. For many researchers, this means shaping transcripts according to empirical needs. For instance, if a data recording involves long stretches of silence, then the researcher should attempt to transcribe this feature of interaction. However, if having long stretches of silence in a transcript is not important to carrying out a particular study, then the issue of accuracy should be redefined accordingly. In other words, accuracy in the representation of talk and interaction is closely related to research traditions, aims, and interests (see Chapter 2). A researcher working in one tradition and with one methodology will have a different understanding of an accurate representation of talk and interaction than other researchers working in, and with, different traditions and methodologies. Notwithstanding variation in theoretical and methodological principles, do transcripts provide a medium that is conducive to accurate representations of talk and interaction?

In order to answer this question, it is important to first identify the types of data collected for research on talk and interaction. Two types of communication data are commonly used to investigate talk and interaction. The first type is referred to as observational data. Observational data are captured *in situ*, as the communicative event unfolds, with an audio and/or video recorder. The recordings (and sometimes field notes) are then later converted into a more reader-friendly transcript. The second type of communication data is commonly known as intuition data. Intuition data sometimes come from the researcher. That is, the researcher invents communicative acts and events to fit the needs of his or her research aims and interests. Intuition data can also come from the researched. That is, research participants are asked how they talk and interact in various settings and situations.

When observational data are juxtaposed with intuition data, it is easy to understand why transcripts are relatively accurate representations of talk and interaction. While both observational and intuition data are temporally displaced communicative artifacts, the latter type of data is more susceptible to inaccuracies because of this displacement. For example, asking a group of students how they interact in class requires them to think back to the numerous encounters they have had with their teachers and classmates. Representation through intuition is susceptible to imprecision because it relies solely on the research participants' memory, perception, and emotions, to name a few, all of which are known to fluctuate. On the other hand, representation through observation is less susceptible to fluctuation and imprecision, as it is based on static – albeit selective – records of past events.

Despite the clear advantage transcripts have over intuition data with regard to the issue of accuracy, transcripts rely on the commitment and knowledge of the researcher to accurately transcribe talk and interaction. Without this commitment and knowledge, transcripts are no more accurate than intuition data. Furthermore, although in theory transcripts are the more accurate form of representation, in practice this is difficult to achieve. The aim of the following chapters is to present and discuss the knowledge and skills necessary to create detailed and accurate transcripts of talk and interaction (see Appendix D, for a quick start guide to transcribing).

CHAPTER 2

Theoretical issues

2.1 Introduction

Researchers working with transcripts to conduct research must make a number of different decisions regarding how best to represent their data recordings. Levels of granularity, the use of special phonetic alphabets, and even the spacing between lines, are some of the many issues that researchers must address whilst transcribing communication data. These issues, and the decisions that are made by researchers transcribing communication data, reflect theoretical assumptions (Ochs, 1979; Duranti, 2006), and possess political and ethical implications. This chapter will discuss these issues and provide references for further reading.

2.2 Transcript as research construct

Transcripts of talk and interaction are commonly used in the social and human sciences to assist in the analysis of data. Researchers create transcripts to generate empirical findings and share analytic observations. The interdependent nature of transcript and data analysis means that the process of transcribing talk and interaction is laden with theoretical issues. Some of these theoretical issues relate to how transcripts are organized, whether the interactants are placed in columns or rows, and the direction in which the text is read, to name a few (Ochs, 1979). While organizational issues are important to the transcription process (see Chapter 3), the present discussion will focus on why data analysis methodologies are an important aspect of producing transcripts. Put differently, this section discusses transcripts as a practice that is inextricably tied to doing research.

A transcript is a research construct because it is created through the analytic lens of a data analysis methodology. Decisions regarding what to include in a transcript, and how to represent talk and interaction in written and/or visual form, are made according to academic and personal interests and biases, as well as what a data analysis methodology is capable of investigating. Therefore, a transcript is neither atheoretical nor completely free of predisposition. Subjectivity in transcripts will, and indeed should, exist (see Section 2.3). While space does not allow a discussion of how transcripts vary according to specific data analysis methodologies

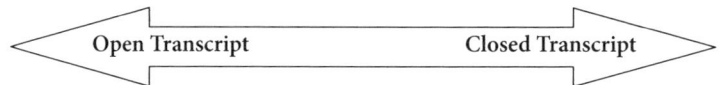

Figure 2.1 Transcription continuum

(for examples of different transcript types, see Schiffrin, Tannen, & Hamilton, 2003; Wetherell, Taylor, & Yates, 2001), it should be noted that any given approach to transcription can be placed on a continuum where both ends represent a different set of methodological issues. Figure 2.1 provides a graphical overview of this continuum.

An open transcript is a result of transcribing talk and interaction as it unfolds at the site of communication. 'Every' feature of talk and interaction is transcribed in order to fully capture what is heard and seen in the data recording. Put differently, no a priori assumptions are made with regard to what features of talk and interaction are important, and should therefore be transcribed. The aim in creating an open transcript is to begin the analytic process with the data recording, rather than a research question, theory, and/or hypothesis. For example, a researcher would not formulate a research question (e.g., do discourse markers promote language comprehension?), and transcribe only those features of talk and interaction that are important to carrying out the research. An open transcript allows researchers to transcribe data recordings with little analytic prejudice; that is, the researcher produces the transcript holistically, and with little preconception of what is and what is not important in the data. This is sometimes called 'unmotivated looking' (ten Have, 2007). One benefit in creating an open transcript is that the higher level of detail allows other researchers to discover potentially important issues and themes that were overlooked by the original transcriber/researcher. Data analysis methodologies that attempt to create an open transcript include, but are not limited to, conversation analysis and discursive psychology (see Hutchby & Wooffitt, 2008; Edwards & Potter, 1992). However, as it is impossible to fully capture every minute detail of talk and interaction (see Section 1.2), transcripts are never truly and completely open.

A closed transcript, on the other hand, is a result of transcribing talk and interaction according to predetermined investigatory aims. Time is spent capturing only those features of talk and interaction that are deemed interesting and relevant, rather than attempting to fully represent what is heard and seen in the data recording. With closed transcripts, a priori assumptions are made concerning what features of talk and interaction are important. A closed transcript seeks to gloss over features of talk and interaction that are believed to fall outside the analytic remit of the adopted data analysis methodology. That is to say, the aim in creating a closed transcript is to selectively highlight only those features of talk

Chapter 2. Theoretical issues **13**

and interaction that assist in the analysis of data. Because closed transcripts are a result of 'selective looking', they are often used to code and quantify features of talk and interaction (see Bloom, 1993; Lampert & Ervin-Tripp, 1993; Slobin, 1993).

The two ends of the continuum demonstrate the need to understand the role transcripts play in research. Transcripts should not be seen as documents that are independent of personal, methodological, and/or disciplinary interests. They are created, whether open or closed or somewhere in between, because of an empirical objective. Identifying and understanding an empirical objective, and knowing what data analysis methodology will help achieve this empirical objective, is an important first step in the transcription process (for a quick start guide to transcribing, see Appendix D). Each data analysis methodology possesses a set of theoretical assumptions that in turn shapes the ways in which a transcript is produced. For instance, unmotivated looking, an analytic idea that is often associated with conversation analysis, requires using a transcript that falls on the open side of the continuum. This is because unmotivated looking requires greater transcription detail, as every feature of talk and interaction is potentially relevant. The empirical objective is to let the data and transcript speak for itself. This, in turn, requires generating a transcript that contains the most micro levels of detail. For instance, in Extract 1, the transcript includes precisely-timed pauses (lines 64, 68, and 70), quiet speech (line 65), overlapping talk (lines 66 and 67), and intonational contours (lines 65, 66, and 67), to name a few (for transcription conventions, see Appendix B).

```
(1)  64                    (1.5)
     65   Peter:            °(okay)° can- can↓ we↑ get one
     66                     [so it's not like] that?
     67   Merchant:         [oh >okay. okay.>]
     68   Peter:            if you don't mind (1.0)
     69                     a:nd, what's the price for them
     70                     (1.0)
```

While it is unlikely that every reader will find these transcribed features of talk and interaction analytically useful, the attention to detail creates a larger canvas of data to examine. In other words, the detail in an open transcript offers a greater range of analytically observable information. Conversely, in Extract 2, the closed transcript does not lend itself to unmotivated looking, as there are less analyzable features of talk and interaction.

```
(2)  65   Peter:            okay can we get one
     66                     so it's not like that
     67   Merchant:         oh okay
     68   Peter:            if you don't mind
     69                     and what's the price for them
```

In this 'cleaned up' version, a researcher can analyze the content of the utterances, but not how the interactants deliver their speech (e.g., prosodic features). While many researchers claim that capturing speech delivery is necessary for understanding spoken communication, a researcher's investigatory aim and/or intended audience may not require prosodic features included in transcripts. For example, it is not uncommon for researchers to present their data recordings and transcripts to a non-academic audience – say a group of teachers – with no specialized knowledge of transcripts and transcript-based analyses. Furthermore, if the analytic aim is to examine the content of utterances, then it could be argued that Extract 1 is superfluous, both in terms of the time needed to transcribe the micro prosodic details, and what the transcript has to offer in terms of achieving the intended research objective.

It should be clear from Extracts 1 and 2 that data analysis methodologies and research aims and interests will influence the content and appearance of transcripts. Good transcription work not only involves knowing the reasons why a transcript should be organized in a particular way (see Chapter 3), but also being aware of the role transcripts play in the larger task of conducting research. That is, transcripts assist in both the representation and analysis of communication data. These two aspects of doing research are informed by, and vary according to, the type of data analysis methodology used. Consequently, the decisions that are made during the process of transcribing talk and interaction must purposefully reflect an empirical objective. Yet because there is no single way of examining communication data, transcripts vary, sometimes greatly, from one data analysis methodology to another.

2.3 Transcript variation

It should be no surprise that transcript variation exists. Researchers are highly susceptible to changes in investigatory aims and interests. Researchers are susceptible to such changes because their knowledge evolves over time, leading them to a better understanding and appreciation of empirical issues. At the same time, the empirical issues researchers investigate may change according to varying interests, what is currently a fashionable area of research, or even personal and institutional obligations. As researchers' knowledge evolves, so too do their empirical interests. Researchers' empirical interests can, of course, influence the type of knowledge they generate. The upshot is that changes in knowledge and interests have an immediate and direct impact on the transcription process. In other words, the complex interplay – between knowledge and interests, and time and affect – influences the decisions that are made with regard to what appears on a transcript. As Duranti

(2006, p. 307) puts it, over time, transcripts grow and evolve into different objects of inquiry.

> "...transcripts have a life or, rather, we give them a life. Transcripts are born, get longer and fatter, and change in character, sometimes through our revisions, other times by simply sitting in a drawer for a few years. When we pick them up again, they read differently" Duranti (2006, p. 307).

Variation and change is a natural process of transcribing communication data, but it should not be taken for granted. Researchers must be cognizant of how their evolving interests and understandings of empirical issues change the way they approach the task of transcribing and analyzing communication data. While it is understood that transcripts vary according to, for example, the data analysis methodology used to investigate a particular phenomenon, this understanding is not well documented. This section will discuss how transcripts vary, and introduce arguments for and against transcript variation.

A transcript is not only a representation of communication data, but also a reflection of the person who created it, what features of talk and interaction he or she is interested in, and the human and technological resources available to this person during the transcription process. In this sense, transcription work is similar to painting a picture. Transcribing and painting both involve transforming an object from one medium to another. What is ultimately produced as the finished product will vary according to a number of different representational decisions. In the case of transcribing, representational decisions relate to how researchers visually and textually depict the seeing and hearing of communication data. For instance, any given stretch of multimodal communication requires seeing what the interactants are doing and listening to what they are saying. Transcripts vary not only because decisions must be made concerning how much of what is seen and heard will be transcribed, but also because any given stretch of communication can be interpreted in different ways.

Laughter, for example, may be interpreted as a sign of being humorous, nervous, or reprehensible, to name a few. The way researchers interpret or hear laughter will in turn influence how the phenomenon appears on their transcripts (see Jefferson, 1985). Transcribing laughter, as with all features of talk and interaction, also requires meticulous listening. Meticulous listening not only involves the ability to distinguish between phonetically similar sounds (e.g., 'haha' and 'hehe'), but also high levels of commitment and involvement in the transcription process. As with many things in life, abilities, commitment, and involvement vary from one researcher to another. Take abilities, for example; researchers possess different levels of proficiency in the transcribed language and years of transcription experience and training. A researcher educated in identifying pitch contours may hear sounds differently than a researcher who lacks this training. In a similar vein, a researcher who speaks English as a second language may hear sounds differently than a researcher who speaks it as a third. These individual differences, among many others, have a significant impact on how transcripts are produced, and are some of the reasons why transcript variation exists.

Another way of capturing the influence individual differences have on transcript variation is to think of skills, abilities, experience, training, and so on, as variables that are situated in the practice of producing transcripts. A researcher makes a number of different representational decisions whilst transcribing. Sometimes these decisions are based on practical constraints (e.g., outdated equipment or deadlines); in other instances, they are made because of theoretical predispositions (e.g., phonological variation and speech therapy or turn-construction units and conversation analysis). Whatever the reasons are, decisions are guided by 'professional vision' (Goodwin, 1994), a term that refers to the unique disciplinary practices involved in seeing, listening, and transcribing communication data for specific audiences and purposes (see also Ashmore, MacMillan, & Brown, 2004). A researcher may use professional vision to determine which, if any, specialized software will be used to play back and transcribe data recordings, how much detail will be included in a transcript, what features of talk and interaction will be coded and/or highlighted, and whether other researchers will assist in the transcription process. While many other transcription issues exist and are influenced by professional vision, the point to be taken from these examples is that transcripts vary because transcribing and analyzing communication data requires making representational decisions that are inextricably tied to investigatory aims.

While few would argue that transcripts are atheoretical, homogenous documents detached from disciplinary aims and interests, conflicting opinions exist regarding whether transcript variation is problematic. On the one hand, transcripts are treated as problematic tools of doing research because they are not reliably produced (Kerswill & Wright, 1990; Bailey, Tillery, & Andres, 2005), and unable to capture the dynamic nature of talk and interaction (Cook, 1990). For some disciplines concerned with phonetic descriptions (e.g., sociolinguistics), transcript variation poses a serious threat to research validity. The phonetic difference between a long and short vowel, for example, has significant implications for researchers working with language variation and change. For these researchers, transcript variation must be monitored and controlled. Other researchers implicitly treat transcript variation as problematic by testing for reliability and searching for ways to maximize inter-transcriber agreement (e.g., Roberts & Robinson, 2004; see also Pitt, Johnson, Hume, Kiesling, Raymond, 2005). Roberts and Robinson (2004), for example, examined the ability of transcribers to reliably represent the same phenomena with a single set of transcription conventions.

On the other hand, transcript variation is seen as normal (cf. Bucholtz, 2007), or at least normal in the sense that transcripts are inextricably tied "to the context of their production and to the practical purposes of their accomplishment" (Mondada, 2007, p. 810). In other words, transcribing talk and interaction is a highly indexical, situated practice that is constantly in a state of flux (see also Duranti, 2006). Variation exists because countless decisions must be made according to research aims and interests. These decisions have less to do with being right or wrong, and more to do with conforming to disciplinary norms and expectations. Consequently, there are no remedies for transcript variation, as there are innumerable ways in which transcript-based research can be done. That is not to say, however, that transcript variation is unproblematic. The process of reducing speech to writing alone raises many problematic issues (see Cook, 1990). Rather, a debate regarding transcript variation should be used to raise awareness of the choices made during transcription work, and the implications these choices have in doing research (Bucholtz, 2007; Mondada, 2007).

Taking both sides of the debate into account, transcript variation is potentially problematic, though there are different understandings of how to address this 'problem'. As noted above, some researchers attempt to control transcript variation, while others use it as an opportunity to reflect on the highly situationally dependent nature of transcription work. One way forward in this debate is to think of transcription work as serving a primary/target audience. Though transcripts are sometimes disseminated for, and viewed by, researchers with diverse disciplinary backgrounds, there is generally a specific target audience for which the transcript is produced. The target audience, say a community of dialectologists, will have specific disciplinary norms and expectations, and empirical aims and interests. Disciplinary and empirical issues in turn create specific transcription requirements. These requirements may differ significantly from, say a community of conversation analysts. Although both communities of researchers may struggle to make use of each other's transcripts, this should not be seen as problematic. Transcripts are highly specialized, situated documents that cannot be standardized to fit the aims and interests of all social and human scientists. It could be said, for this reason, that variation across disciplines is less problematic than variation within. In fact, researchers who attempt to test and control transcript variation do so for the purpose of a specific target audience (e.g., for the conversation analytic community, see Roberts & Robinson, 2004; for the dialectology community, see Bailey, Tillery, & Andres, 2005). In other words, these researchers do not attempt to control transcript variation in order to create a homogenized transcript for all to read and use. With these issues in mind, a researcher should always refer to the conventions used by other researchers working in the same discipline in order to understand what is good/accepted transcription practice.

2.4 Transcription politics

The two previous sections reviewed the reasons why researchers make representational decisions, and discussed how these decisions affect transcript variation. The issues that underpin representational decisions were identified to raise awareness of the highly theoretical nature of transcription work, and not to argue that one transcription approach or decision is better than another. While the theoretical issues identified thus far highlight the need to be more reflective about the disciplinary reasons why transcripts vary, it is also crucial to understand the impact transcripts have on the people transcribed.

Transcripts not only represent approximations of talk and interaction, they also convey an enormous amount of information regarding the interactants under investigation. For instance, the frequency and ways in which troubles in communication are repaired and corrected may say something about the relationship of the interactants (e.g., Hall, 2007), or the management of topics may reveal power struggles and institutional roles (e.g., Maynard, 1991). Researchers have an incredible amount of power at their disposal, as they determine how the words spoken by, for example, patients, students, or family members, are presented to a larger audience. The power researchers possess is even more apparent when the interactants are vulnerable and underrepresented members of society or affiliated with institutions of authority, discussing highly personal and/or sensitive issues. In such scenarios, even the smallest representational decision may have serious consequences for those transcribed. The decision, for example, to omit a word or highlight a specific utterance, may change the way an audience interprets the dynamics of the setting and interactants under investigation. Bucholtz (2000), for example, discusses in detail how the omission of utterances in a transcript for a criminal case depicted a police officer as caring and supportive, while her own version of the transcript, which included the missing utterances, showed that the police officer was coercive and self-seeking. Therefore, the interactants that are transcribed should be taken into consideration when making representational decisions (cf. Coulthard, 1996). Roberts (1997, p. 170) eloquently captures this observation by stating "we are transcribing people when we transcribe talk."

The political consequences of transcribing talk and interaction is perhaps most relevant when decisions are made regarding the accuracy of capturing speech styles and dialectal varieties. The interactants that are transcribed are more than the names given to them on a transcript. The interactants not only have unique life histories, emotions, thoughts, and personalities, but also particular ways in which they pronounce sounds, construct sentences, and participate in communication. The researcher is left with the difficult challenge in determining how to represent the interactants' storied and colorful ways of communicating. One way of capturing

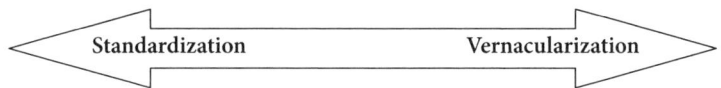

Figure 2.2 Representation continuum

the communicative styles of interactants is to transcribe the talk as it is being spoken. This approach is referred to as vernacularization. However, some researchers argue that vernacularization is socially problematic (see below), and thus suggest researchers to transcribe the words spoken by interactants according to standard written orthography. This approach is referred to as standardization. Vernacularization and standardization form two sides of a continuum. This continuum is graphically presented in Figure 2.2.

Vernacularization seeks to capture the unique ways and styles in which words and utterances are spoken. This approach aims to provide a written representation of regional dialects, colloquial features of talk (i.e., slang), and unique accents.

Because words and utterances are often spoken differently than they are written, researchers must decide whether and to what degree they will be faithful to what Jefferson (1983) calls the 'pronunciational particulars' of interactants. Pronunciational particulars are spoken words and utterances that deviate from standard spelling. Pronunciational particulars carry social markers – as is the case, for example, with regional varieties (e.g., New York English) – so it is often necessary to capture words and utterances as they are spoken in order to reflect the identities of the interactants.

Researchers have two transcribing options for vernacularization. The first option is to use non-standard spelling. For instance, in Extract 3, Chris' utterance has been transcribed using non-standard spelling in order to highlight the colloquial manner in which he asks a question, and to somewhat accurately represent the pronunciation of the spoken words.

```
(3)   53              (12.0)
      54   Chris:     wht'she lukin for? (.) anarchy?=
      55   Merchant:  =(* *)
```

The non-standard spelling option is sometimes referred to as 'eye dialect' or 'orthographic metonymy' (see Bucholtz, 2000, p. 1455). The second option of vernacularization is to use the International Phonetic Alphabet to phonetically capture pronunciational particulars. So, for example, 'did'ya see dat' would be transcribed as 'did [jʊː] see [dæ]t'. While both vernacularization options provide reasonably accurate depictions of pronunciational particulars, there are different justifications for using each option. For researchers working with accents and dialects (e.g., sociolinguists and dialectologists), the International Phonetic Alphabet is used because it is believed to provide a technically/scientifically reliable way of capturing pronunciational particulars. However, some would argue that the precision provided by this approach is misguided because many people in the academic community lack the specialized training necessary to decode such transcripts. At a practical level, learning and applying the International Phonetic Alphabet takes many months, if not years, to master. Alternatively, non-standard spelling is used because this option does not require special training, is accessible to a wider audience, and adds a folksy, personal touch to the transcribed words and utterances.

While non-standard spelling is indeed more accessible and literarily appealing, eye dialect is not without its problems. For instance, spelling words and utterances as they are spoken may lead to negative social evaluations of the interactants (Preston, 1985). Non-standard spelling may be interpreted as defective speech, rather than a true and accurate representation of spoken communication. As a result, a fine balance exists between capturing pronunciational particulars and caricaturizing the interactants under investigation. This is especially true when transcribing non-native speakers of a language or members of a particular speech community (e.g., African American Vernacular English). Because there are widespread assumptions regarding the 'non-standardness' of the language spoken by these interactants, eye dialect may reinforce stereotypical assumptions (Jaffe & Walton, 2000). It should be noted that while the International Phonetic Alphabet may capture pronunciational particulars without the danger of cartoon representations, it may exoticize the interactants' speech in an equally socially detrimental manner (Bucholtz, 2000).

On the other side of the continuum is standardization. Standardization seeks to transcribe spoken words and utterances in standard written orthography. So, for example, 'did'ya see dat' would be transcribed as 'did you see that', or 'wht'she lukin for?' in Extract 3 would be transcribed as 'what is she looking for?' (see Extract 4).

```
(4)  53                (12.0)
     54   Chris:       what is she looking for?
     55                (.) anarchy?=
     56   Merchant:    =(* *)
```

While standardization may not lead to cartoon and exotic representations of the interactants, it too is not without its problems. Standardizing words and utterances is problematic, as it strips away the idiosyncrasies of communication, and reduces the interactants to generic social beings. Furthermore, standardized words and utterances carry less social-interactional information, and this is potentially problematic, as researchers are limited in what they can do analytically with the transcript. For example, transcribing 'did'ya see dat' in standard written orthography strips away potentially important analytic information pertaining to who the interactants are, where they come from, and what speech communities they belong to, to name a few. In addition, standardization requires making theoretically informed decisions regarding which spoken variety will be deemed non-standard, and thus represented in standard written orthography. These decisions require extensive socio-historical knowledge of the language and interactants. Attaining such knowledge requires many years of training with, and/or first-hand knowledge of, the language spoken by the interactants under investigation. Accordingly, reasons for standardizing pronunciational particulars will vary from one speech community to another, and indeed from one investigatory aim to another.

As with all continuums, choosing one approach to representing the talk and interaction of the interactants does not mean that the other cannot be used. Researcher can, and should, be selective and strategic in their decisions to represent the talk and interaction in a particular way. For instance, some researchers vernacularize only when the pronunciation particulars are made relevant by the interactants. If a pronunciation particular leads to miscommunication, for example, then the researcher will use either the International Phonetic Alphabet or non-standard spelling to highlight the source of communication trouble. Conversely, standardization can be used selectively and strategically if the researcher has political motives for wanting to limit stereotypical evaluations of the interactants. For instance, a researcher may want to make morphological changes to certain words in order to avert readers from casting judgement on the proficiency of an interactant (e.g., adding the past tense *-ed* when it is omitted or used incorrectly). The challenge for the researcher is to not only determine when to use vernacularization or standardization, but to also understand that representational decisions are inherently political because they have real world implications for the interactants under investigation.

2.5 Transcription ethics

As with any research-related activity dealing with humans, transcribing talk and interaction requires following ethical guidelines. Has permission been granted to record, transcribe, and disseminate personal information? Is it necessary to mask people and place names with pseudonyms? What are the differences between informed and written consent? Should transcripts be given to those that are transcribed? While detailed ethical information regarding research conduct is available from a number of different sources (e.g., professional organizations, university regulations, and institution guidelines), it is likely that these sources say little – if anything at all – with regard to the ethics of transcribing communication data. Although this section does not attempt to provide or review ethical guidelines, important procedural information pertaining to the ethics of transcribing will be discussed. Specifically, this section will discuss how researchers prepare transcripts when dealing with sensitive and/or confidential data.

After ethical clearance has been given to collect data, it is important to consider how the people and places named in transcripts are presented. A common way of safeguarding the identity of the interactants under investigation is to present them as letters or numbers or a combination of both. For example, compare Extracts 5 and 6. In Extract 5, the interactants are identified by name.

```
(5)  157   Chris:    [how much are you paying for it?
     158   Peter:    tw[enty five
```

In Extract 6, Chris and Peter are represented as speaker 1 (S1) and speaker 2 (S2), respectively.

```
(6)  157   S1:    [how much are you paying for it?
     158   S2:    tw[enty five
```

Using letter-number combinations is common practice, as they completely mask the identity of the interactants. In addition, letter-number combinations are relatively easy to apply with the 'find' and 'replace' functions that are present in most word processing software programs. More importantly, letter-number combinations do not impose a single category on the interactants (e.g., teacher and student or doctor and patient), as is the case when using institutional labels in lieu of real names. In dyadic interaction, letter-number combinations are also relatively easy to follow; that is, they do not take a significant amount of effort to determine who is saying what in a transcript.

However, in multi-party interaction, say in a classroom or at a dinner table, letter-number combinations are less effective in providing an easy-to-follow format for readers. It is much easier to keep track of a multi-party communicative event when the interactants are identified by name. Furthermore, some data analysis methodologies require transcribing the delivery of talk according to stress and intonation (e.g., conversation analysis). If it is necessary to investigate and describe the delivery of talk, then letter-number combinations should not be used. For instance, compare the fictitious exchanges in Extracts 7 and 8. In Extract 7, the names are included in the transcript.

```
(7)  1   Melissa:   can you take out the garbage?
     2   Bob:       no, Melissa, I cannot
```

Note the stress placed in Bob's delivery of 'Melissa' and 'cannot'. It could be said that Bob is strengthening his refusal by stressing both the name of the recipient and his unwillingness to take out the garbage. Compare this example with Extract 8, where the recipient's name has been replaced with a letter-number combination.

(8) 1   S1:   can you take out the garbage?
     2   S2:   no, S1, I cannot

While it is still possible to see that S2 (Bob) is addressing his recipient by name, the letter-number combination does not allow the researcher to transcribe where the stressed is placed in the spoken name. Furthermore, the letter-number combination does not have the same literary impact as Extract 7. Extract 8 requires more imagination on the reader's part to mentally visualize that S1 is in fact a name that is being spoken with syllable initial stress. A more significant problem with using letter-number combinations is that the interactants under investigation are reduced to a series of letters and numbers. Using 'Melissa' as a pseudonym, conversely, in lieu of 'S1', brings life to the communicative exchange whilst masking the identity of the interactant. Pseudonyms are helpful in reminding readers that transcripts represent the utterances spoken by real people with storied lives, rather than words and utterances devoid of social meaning. Pseudonyms can be created in many ways, so no comprehensive list will be provided here. Examples include, but are not limited to, using the first letter of the real name, as in 'Craig' for 'Chris', or using the same number of syllables, as in 'Jackson' for 'Freddy'. The latter approach is particularly helpful when transcribing speech delivery. Other approaches that are helpful in selecting pseudonyms that retain important social markers while maintaining anonymity include using names that represent the same gender and ethnicity of the interactants under investigation. While many suggestions and reasons can be given for using a particular approach, a researcher's main priority in using pseudonyms is to safeguard anonymity. Pseudonyms must not provide any information that may potentially reveal the true identities of the interactants.

However, transcribing data from an open domain (e.g., a radio broadcast or a YouTube video) does not typically require masking identities, as the interactants have already publically identified themselves. Nevertheless, ethical variation is likely to exist with regard to what extent data is considered public or private, so it is important to consult an ethical committee for guidance. Seeking ethical advice is especially important in researching digital media and communication, as social networking sites like Facebook and Twitter blur the boundaries between public and private.

If place names must be changed because of ethical reasons, then pseudonyms should be used according to the same guidelines and for the same reasons discussed previously for personal names. However, some place names do not require pseudonyms because they are sufficiently ambiguous, as with large geographical areas (e.g., Africa, South Korea, UK). Conversely, some place names are too unique or distinct to remain unchanged (e.g., institutions, small towns, cities).

When presenting or disseminating data at a conference or workshop, it is important to use pseudonyms when discussing sensitive and/or confidential information pertaining to, and contained in, the transcript. In other words, when presenting data to the academic community, researchers should not use real people and place names, even if the transcripts are anonymized. Researchers can avoid this situation by selecting pseudonyms before beginning the transcription process, and conditioning themselves to use these fictitious names when referring to their data recordings. In a similar vein, researchers should take steps to safeguard the identity of the interactants when playing back data recordings at conferences and workshops. This suggestion is especially important, as it is not uncommon for researchers to use pseudonyms in their transcripts, only to realize that their data recordings reveal people and place names. Researchers can prevent this problem from occurring by using an audio playback program to create white noise over any instances of talk that reveal information that should be anonymized (for a discussion of how to manipulate media in order to conceal the identity of the interactants in video recordings, see Section 5.3).

CHAPTER 3

Transcribing talk and interaction
The basics

3.1 Introduction

The last two chapters discussed what transcripts of talk and interaction are, how they are used, and the theoretical issues that underpin the representation of communication data. The previous chapter in particular identified the reasons why detailed transcripts of verbal and nonverbal communication are particularly important for researchers concerned with communication, discussed issues of accuracy, and finally identified the ethical and theoretical implications of transcribing and disseminating transcripts of talk and interaction. Now that a theoretical foundation has been established, it is important to discuss the practicalities of producing transcripts.

This chapter will focus on the fundamentals of converting recordings of communication data to a text-based document that is suitable for presentation and dissemination. These fundamentals are broken into three issues (see Table 3.1). The issues address most of what a researcher needs to take into consideration when beginning the task of transcribing data recordings (for a quick start guide to transcribing, see Appendix D).

It is important to note that these three issues do not imply that transcribing requires following a specific sequence. Although organizational issues are generally dealt with before anything is actually transcribed (Issue 2), as a transcript-based researcher, playing back data (Issue 1), and addressing issues related to content (Issue 3), is a cyclical process. This chapter assumes that the reader is in possession of data recordings. In other words, this chapter does not discuss how researchers should (or could) go about collecting data recordings. The suggestions provided below are related to the decisions that researchers make as they consider how best to transform their data recordings into a text-based document. For each decision made, there are practical and theoretical reasons for using a

Table 3.1 Basic transcription issues

Issue 1	*Playback*	e.g., software and hardware related transcription issues
Issue 2	*Organization*	e.g., layout, line numbers, line breaks, spacing, and placement
Issue 3	*Content*	e.g., font type, speaker representation, and transcription detail

particular format, font, or line-numbering system, for example. Even the layout of transcripts has important theoretical and practical implications. Furthermore, the suggestions made, and transcription guidelines provided, in this, and subsequent chapters, highlight the laborious nature of transcription work. It is important to note here – at the outset of this chapter – that transcribing data recordings – even with basic orthographic conventions (i.e., transcribing words and utterances with no speech delivery markers) – requires hours upon hours of meticulous work in front of a computer. These suggestions and guidelines are not intended to make the transcribing process unnecessarily complex, but to provide readers with the knowledge and tools to appropriately address the important, but challenging task of transcribing communication data.

3.2 Playback

It would be an understatement to claim that the task of transcribing talk and interaction requires playing back segments of data recordings. A 10-minute recording of two interactants communicating on a standard telephone (i.e., no nonverbal communication) can take several hours, if not more, to transcribe verbatim. Many more additional hours are required to transcribe the paralinguistic features of talk (which includes prosody), and pauses within and between utterances (see Chapter 4). This is because it is not humanly possible to transcribe at the same speed as a data recording is played. Researchers frequently stop their data recordings in order to type the spoken utterances, depict any important nonverbal movements, and represent pauses if necessary, only to rewind and repeat the process numerous times until the transcript closely represents the recorded talk and interaction. Accordingly, a crucial aspect of transcription work is playing back data recordings. Researchers must be familiar with the tools that are used to deal with this part of the transcription process.

In previous years, analogue media players and stopwatches were used to play back and transcribe communication data. Transcribing communication data with these tools meant painstakingly searching for, and timing, segments of talk and interaction. Fortunately, in these times, more efficient and effective software programs are used for these transcription tasks. Today there are several free, open-source computer programs that help researchers with the many tasks related to transcribing communication data. Rather than identify and provide reviews of these programs (for an overview of transcription software, see Section 6.3.6), this section will explain what features/tools are essential for playing back data recordings. The discussion below assumes that the data recording that must be transcribed has been, or is, digitized, and is in a standard audio file format (e.g., MP3 or WAV).

3.2.1 Software issues

The single most helpful feature in playing back data is perhaps the ability of a program to represent data recordings as sound waves, as shown in Figure 3.1.

Most programs that depict data recordings in sound waves allow researchers to highlight segments of speech, as shown in Figure 3.2.

The ability to highlight a sound wave has two key benefits. First, the highlighting feature can be used to play and replay a segment of speech in isolation (i.e., looping), without the need to repeatedly search for its beginning and end points (cf. analogue media players). This is particularly helpful in locating the beginning and end points of overlapping talk, for example. Furthermore, if a smaller segment of talk is difficult to transcribe because of, for example, overlapping talk or laughter, then the highlighting feature will save valuable transcription time in that the highlighted area can be played in a loop until the segment in question is transcribed. In other words, a researcher's hands are completely free from playing, stopping, and rewinding the data recording, which in turn allows the researcher to focus on the task of transcribing the segment in question. Second, most programs that have the ability to highlight segments of speech will also generate the total duration of the highlighted area. The benefit here is that pauses, if required in the transcript, are timed up to the nearest millionths of a second. Precise timings can also be used to provide contextual background information for transcripts during dissemination and/or for publication, as well as bookmarking phenomena that will be transcribed and/or analyzed at a later date.

Figure 3.1 Sound wave

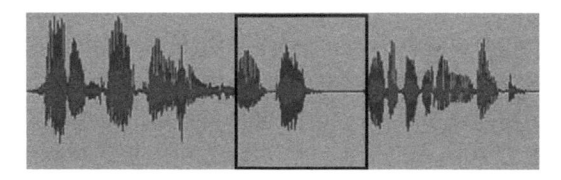

Figure 3.2 Highlighting a sound wave

The second most helpful feature in playing back data recordings is the ability to manipulate the sound of communication. Two sub-features of sound manipulation are especially beneficial: speed and background noise. First, data recordings are notoriously difficult to transcribe. Recording equipment is sometimes misplaced, leading to muffled sounds and incomprehensible conversations. In other recording situations, the interactants may be whispering, speaking with thick accents, using unfamiliar vernacular, or talking over each other, to name a few. The benefit in manipulating the sound of communication is that data recordings can be sped up or slowed down in order to create a more comprehensible data recording. The degree to, and ease in which, a researcher can speed up or down the data recording will vary according to the program used, though most playback programs offer some ability to manipulate the sound of communication. As this feature is invaluable to the transcription process, it is recommended that several playback programs are tested and compared for ease of use and effectiveness. Second, the ability to reduce and eliminate background noise is helpful when extraneous sounds in the data recording hinder comprehensibility. For example, hissing noises from poorly recorded data can be eliminated in a matter of seconds. The ability to reduce or eliminate extraneous sounds will not only make the transcription process more enjoyable, but an audience will also find listening to the data less of a chore if, and when, the data recording is shared to the academic community.

3.2.2 Hardware issues

In addition to software features, there are two hardware issues that should be taken into consideration when playing back data recordings. The first, and most important, hardware issue concerns the way in which sounds are emitted when playing back data recordings. On the one hand, a high quality set of speakers that produces a wide-range of frequency sounds will provide the benefit of playing back data recordings in stereo surround sound, a condition that many argue is the most conducive for listening to recordings of data. Speakers also offer the opportunity to play back data recordings in situations when more than one person is listening and/or transcribing, as in cases when difficult to comprehend utterances require the assistance of colleagues. On the other hand, the sound emitted from high quality headphones is not subjected to the type of sound distortions that may exist when playing back data recordings with speakers in spaces other than sound rooms – that is to say, many rooms are built in a way that muffles the sounds emitted from speakers. Furthermore, headphones provide the obvious benefit of playing back data in privacy. Higher quality headphones also reduce outside noise, which can prove helpful when transcribing in public spaces (e.g., doctoral study room). As the quality of sound emitted from speakers and headphones varies greatly, it is good practice to test several models, as well as both options, before choosing one.

The second hardware issue relates to how a researcher plays, stops, rewinds, and fast forwards, or in other words, moves through, data recordings. As the transcription process is closely linked to the task of moving through data recordings, it is important to know what playback options are available. The first option in moving through data recordings is to use the stock buttons provided by a software program. This option requires moving the cursor over and clicking the, for example, stop and rewind buttons, in order to move through the data recording. While many researchers are content with using stock buttons to search through data recordings, during long, intensive transcribing sessions, the act of moving the hands away from the keyboard in order to, for example, stop and rewind, is laborious, but more importantly, takes precious time away from the task of transcribing talk and interaction. The second option is to use hotkeys, also known as keyboard shortcuts. The benefit here is that hotkeys are easy to set up and use, and maximizes the time a researcher's hands are on the keyboard. The last option is to purchase USB foot pedals. It is difficult to say whether foot pedals are significantly more efficient than hotkeys. However, for some researchers, transcribing communication data is easier with foot pedals, as the hands are devoted entirely to typing. As with speakers and headphones, all options should be tested and compared before relying on one.

3.3 Organization

Before any features of talk and interaction are transcribed, it is important to consider the overall organization of a transcript. The issues discussed in this section should be read with great consideration, as organizational issues influence how the words and utterances contained in a transcript are read and interpreted by the academic community (see Ochs, 1979; Bucholtz, 2000). The discussion below is predicated on the assumption that the language transcribed is read from left to right and top to bottom, and that a word processing program will be used (for a brief discussion of transcription software, see Section 6.3.6).

3.3.1 Layout

One of the first transcription issues that must be addressed is the visual presentation of a transcript. A well-planned layout will enhance the readability of a transcript by presenting the text in an orderly and visually pleasing way, thus making the task of locating specific segments of talk and interaction more efficient.

The first layout issue to address is margin sizes. Margin sizes play an important role in the readability, usability, and portability of transcripts. For instance, small margins (less than 2.54 cm) provide more space for inputting text. On each page, a researcher has more vertical and horizontal space to input text. This, in turn, decreases the overall length of a transcript (i.e., less page numbers). However, a text-heavy page hinders the readability of a transcript and creates undue stress on the eyes. Conversely, transcripts with large margins restrict the amount of text that can be inputted on each page. Large margins prevent researchers from producing text-heavy transcripts, and provide the space necessary to write analytic notes on all four sides of each page during conferences and data workshops. Transcripts with small margins are less portable in that when the time comes to copy and paste smaller segments of talk and interaction onto a new document – say for the data analysis section of a doctoral dissertation or in a conference handout – the segment of talk and interaction that is pasted is more likely to become distorted because of differences in margin sizes (for a discussion of portability, see also Section 3.3.3). Some publications, for example, require manuscripts to be submitted with very large margins (e.g., more than 3 cm). If the original transcript has been created with small margins (e.g., 1.5 cm), then the pasted segment of talk and interaction must be reformatted in order to fit the new document. Reformatting segments of talk and interaction to fit documents with different margin sizes is a laborious task because the researcher must renumber the pasted segments of talk and interaction (for an example of this, see Section 3.3.3). Because there are no significant advantages in producing transcripts with small margins, it is advisable to use 3 cm (or more) for both the left and right margins.

The next issue to address is speaker layout. Speaker layout refers to where the interactants are located on a transcript. Interactants can be presented in two ways. The first way, referred to as column representation, places speakers on the top of each page. In column representation, each utterance in a column corresponds to one speaker, as in Extract 1.

```
(1)       Chris              Peter            Merchant
      157 [how much are
          you paying for
          it?
      158                    tw[enty five
      159                                     [no::: twenty five
```

With regard to the flow of information in Extract 1, utterances are read from left to right, and top to bottom. The line numbers, which will be discussed below (see Section 3.3.2), are placed on the far left of the transcript, going down sequentially, though some researchers may wish to put the line numbers in speaker columns, as in Extract 2.

```
(2)         Chris                Peter              Merchant
      157   [how much are
            you paying for it?
                                 158 tw[enty five
                                                    159 [no::: twenty five
```

Notwithstanding variation in where line numbers are placed, column representation may be beneficial when data recordings comprise two interactants, say an interviewer and interviewee. In such instances, the visual representation of placing speakers in columns may prove beneficial if the transcribing aim is to demonstrate, for example, that the two roles of the interactants result in different interactional patterns. In other words, columns may help distinguish differences in speaker utterances when two interactants have distinct ways of interacting and/or institutional roles.

Column representation, however, does not provide the most readable transcripts when data recordings comprise three or more speakers, especially when each speaker turn is long in duration. Researchers may also find it difficult to represent overlapping talk (represented as open brackets in the extract below), particularly when three or more speakers are talking at the same time. Following speakership is also potentially difficult when speaker transitions do not move from left to right or even right to left, but rather, as in Extract 3, from the far left column to the far right column and back to the middle column.

```
(3)         Chris                Merchant           Peter
      157   [how much are
            you paying for it?
      158                                           tw[enty five
      159                        [no::: twenty five
```

The last problem with column representation worth mentioning refers back to the issue of margin sizes and portability. Placing speakers in columns requires small margins, which in turn minimizes the portability of transcripts.

The second and most common way of placing speakers in transcripts is referred to as row representation. In row representation, speakers are placed on the left-hand side of each page, and each row of speech corresponds to one speaker, as in Extract 4.

```
(4)   157   Chris:      [how much are you paying for it?
      158   Peter:      tw[enty five
      159   Merchant:   [no::: twenty five
```

It is important to note that there is no need to re-identify the speaker when a long utterance spills over to the next row, as in Extract 5.

(5) 178 Peter: okay so i got forty (.) twenty
    179   (.) twenty ((counting money))
    180 Chris: ooh lots of money
    181 Peter: forty (.) lots. lots↑ of↓ money↑
    182   lots of money and lots of honey
    183   wrapped up in' a five↑pound↓note↑
    184   (2.0)
    185 Merchant: no problem
    186   (2.0)
    187 Peter: thank you::=
    188 Merchant: =i think maybe you're- you're
    189   big boss so small money for you
    190   people

The benefit of using row representation is that there are fewer layout problems when transcribing multi-party interaction. Unlike column representation, placing speakers at the beginning of rows allows for more horizontal transcribing space, as the utterance of one speaker occupies the entire row. Furthermore, having rows represent speakers enhances the readability of transcripts. Readers will find that it is easier to follow speakership when speaker transitions occur linearly, one after the other. Transcripts with row representation are also more portable in that they can be copied and pasted onto documents with little to no need to renumber transcripts and change document settings. The key difference in portability comes from the fact that row representation can be used with different margin sizes, whereas column representation only works well with very small margins.

However, row representation poses some organizational dilemmas. First, placing speakers on the left-hand side of each page requires researchers to decide when each row will end. Should a row end at the completion of a clause, utterance, or turn? Investigatory aims, data analysis methodologies, and research traditions, will dictate when to end a row (for a discussion of transcript as research construct, see Section 2.2), so research handbooks and academic colleagues are the best source of information to determine when to end each row. For example, ending rows at the completion of clauses may be conducive for examining what role grammar plays in spoken interaction, while ending rows at turn transitions benefits researchers investigating turn-taking practices.

A further organizational dilemma relates to where pauses are placed. Are turn-transitional pauses placed in separate rows when two turns at talk are spoken by different speakers or in the same row at the end of the first turn at talk? Placing pauses between two turns at talk spoken by different people allows readers to easily follow speakership and turn transitions, while placing pauses at the end of completed turns produces shorter transcripts for the space conscious researcher.

Despite these organizational dilemmas, the benefits of row representation far outweigh the disadvantages. In addition, because column representation leads to many organizational problems, row representation should be used for most transcription work.

The last layout issue deals with how transcripts are named and later referenced. Whether a transcript represents an entire three-hour recording of communication or a three-minute segment of a longer recording, it is important to adopt a referencing system so that transcripts are easily identified during data dissemination and presentation. A referencing system can include alpha-numerals (e.g., Extract 3a, Extract 3b, Extract 3c, and so on), time stamps (e.g., 7 min 33 sec or 7:33), titles ('cultural exchange'), and any other relevant information that may assist in identification. In Extract 6 below, for example, the extract is identified with alpha-numerals (Market 1), a time stamp (0:55), and a title (Negotiation Opening).

```
(6)  Market 1
     0:55
     Negotiation Opening
     1              (7.2)
     2   Peter:     there it is, it's this way
     3              ((inaudible))
     4              (10.9) ((walking to merchant))
     5   Merchant:  hello sir. (0.5) do↓ you↑
     6              wa↓nna↑ something?
     7              (0.4)
     8   Peter:     walk in here and have a look.
```

The identification sign 'Market' denotes the setting under investigation, whereas the '1' is used in reference to a specific recording number. It is important to note that there is no single way of using alpha-numerals, though all referencing systems should follow some type of sequence. Time stamps are typically placed after the identification of the data recording (Market 1), and the time should include the beginning point (and sometimes end point) of the data recording. The title is perhaps the least commonly used aspect of a referencing system, though some researchers prefer to add them because they make transcripts and data extracts more memorable. Referencing systems are particularly helpful, as they allow researchers to easily to go back to data recordings for subsequent and additional transcribing and analyses sessions. Because transcripts are based on data recordings, the referencing system should correspond to the same name given for the audio-visual files. In other words, it is good practice to have the same name for both transcript and data recording file. Furthermore, researchers often need to create smaller segments of talk and interaction within longer transcripts, especially for research dissemination and publication. Alpha-numerals, time stamps, and titles, will not only help in disseminating research, but a reference system will also make it easier to cross-reference larger transcripts when a collection of smaller segments are taken from different sources.

3.3.2 Line numbers

Transcribing communication data with line numbers is important for many reasons. Whether writing an academic paper or giving a scholarly presentation, transcript-based research requires referring back to specific stretches and features of talk and interaction. Line numbers offer quick identification of specific stretches and features of talk and interaction, provide some indication of how long transcripts are, and when smaller segments of transcripts are used for dissemination and/or publication, they allow researchers to know where, sequentially, the segments fits within a larger transcript.

Line numbers should always correspond to talk and interaction, and not the interactants under investigation. Line numbers that correspond to interactants – while organizationally better than omitting line numbers from transcripts all together – make it difficult for researchers to refer to specific stretches and features of talk and interaction. In Extract 7, for instance, the second half of the merchant's question ('wa↓nna↑ something?'), and the 0.4-second pause that follows, do not have corresponding line numbers, as the line numbers only correspond to the interactants.

```
(7)  5   Merchant:   hello sir. (0.5) do↓ you↑
                     wa↓nna↑ something?
                     (0.4)
     6   Peter:      walk in here and have a look.
```

With this format, a researcher writing or presenting an analysis of Extract 7 has no efficient way of referring to the talk and interaction that has not been numbered. More importantly, anyone reading an analysis or listening to a presentation of Extract 7 will find it difficult to follow references to the second half of the merchant's question and the 0.4-second pause that follows. This is no trivial matter, as a crucial aspect of making good analytic observations is the ability to make precise and clear references to specific stretches of talk and interaction.

Conversely, Extract 8 is referentially more suitable for locating and discussing specific features of talk and interaction.

```
(8)  5   Merchant:   hello sir. (0.5) do↓ you↑
     6               wa↓nna↑ something?
     7               (0.4)
     8   Peter:      walk in here and have a look.
```

Because it is not uncommon for transcripts to include thousands of lines of talk and interaction, many researchers use the auto-numbering feature available in most word processing programs (nb. most transcription programs have this feature as well, but some do not offer the option to transcribe without line numbers). As with all aspects of transcribing, the decision to rely on a word processing program to automatically number transcripts must be based on sound justifications. First, a researcher must determine whether a transcript will be made into smaller segments and put into different documents. This is common practice for research publication and dissemination, where space and time only permit analyses of smaller segments of talk and interaction. If smaller segments will be used, then a researcher should consider inputting the numbers manually, as auto-generated line numbers do not generally copy and paste from one document to another. A considerable amount of time is required re-numbering each smaller segment of talk and interaction and maintaining the original sequence of numbers. If smaller segments will not be used, then the auto-numbering feature will save a considerable amount of transcription time.

3.3.3 Line breaks

The second organizational issue that must be addressed is line breaks. Line breaks are performed by hitting the carriage return/enter key, which in turn ends a current line of talk and interaction and begins a new one. Line breaks are an important transcription issue, as the position of line breaks will shape other organizational issues. For example, early line breaks will result in shorter rows of talk and interaction and more line numbers.

```
(9)  181   Peter:    forty (.) lots. lots↑
     182             of↓ money↑ lots of money
     183             and lots of honey wrapped
     184             up in'a five↑pound↓note↑
     185             (2.0)
```

Conversely, late line breaks will result in longer rows of talk and interaction and less line numbers.

```
(10) 181   Peter:    forty (.) lots. lots↑ of↓ money↑ lots
     182             of money and lots of honey wrapped
     183             up in'a five↑pound↓note↑ (2.0)
```

Transcript length is the most immediately observable consequence of line breaks. Early line breaks result in longer transcripts, whereas late line breaks produce shorter transcripts. Late line breaks increase the (trans)portability of transcripts if full-length hardcopies are made. The overall shorter transcript produced as a result of late line breaks also requires less physical storage space. In addition, shorter transcripts are attractive to some researchers working with strict length restrictions.

However, despite the benefits of late line breaks, early line breaks should be used because they help create a more digitally portable, readable, and usable transcript. For instance, early line breaks increase the portability of transcripts by making it easier to copy and paste smaller segments of talk and interaction from one document to another. This is especially true when both documents contain different margin sizes (see Section 3.3.1). For example, copying and pasting a smaller segment of transcript with late line breaks onto a document with wide page margins will cause havoc to the original numbering system, resulting in additional time spent reformatting and renumbering rows of talk and interaction. Extract 11 illustrates the outcome of copying and pasting talk and interaction with late line breaks onto a document with wide margins.

```
(11) 181   Peter:    forty (.) lots. lots↑ of↓
     money↑ lots of
     182              money and lots of honey wrapped
     up in'a
     183              five↑pound↓note↑(2.0)
```

Extract 11 does not have enough horizontal space to accommodate the pasted transcript. Because longer rows of talk and interaction are split into two, a substantial amount of time is required reformatting and renumbering the new transcript (see Extract 12).

```
(12) 181   Peter:    forty (.) lots. lots↑ of↓
     182              money↑ lots of
     183              money and lots of honey wrapped
     184              up in'a
     185              five↑pound↓note↑(2.0)
```

In order to avoid spending many hours reformatting and renumbering transcripts, early line breaks should be used, but they should also be used with wide margins. That is to say, transcripts should be created with early line breaks, even if each page has been set with wide margins. This is because letting each row of talk and interaction spill over to the next – without hitting the carriage return/enter key – decreases the portability of transcripts in that the new document may interpret each row as a continuous line of communication, leading to the same problem presented in Extract 11. Conversely, ending each row of talk and interaction with the carriage return/enter key creates a document 'marker' that signals to the new document that each line should end at a particular point. In other words, line breaks have a slightly different organizational function than margin sizes. Furthermore, using early line breaks (with wide margins) enhances the readability and usability of transcripts by creating extra 'white space'. The benefit in having large white spaces is that transcript-based research often requires writing analytic notes directly onto hardcopies of transcripts, as is often that case during research presentations and data workshops. A large white space gives researchers the area needed to keep notes without writing over the transcribed data. Furthermore, transcripts with larger white spaces are arguably easier on the eye, as the entire page is not suffocated with text.

Lastly, line breaks are sometimes determined according to what constitutes an utterance. In other words, some researchers begin a new line of talk and interaction if a new utterance begins – even if the new utterance is spoken by the same interactant. While doing so may provide a more systematic approach to transcribing communication data, constructing a workable definition of what constitutes an utterance during spoken interaction is an extremely difficult task. Is an utterance based loosely on grammatical rules? Do pauses constitute ends points of utterances? Are utterances made up of more than one word? Furthermore, even a carefully constructed, theoretically informed definition of utterance will be shaped by the practicalities of transcribing. For instance, margin sizes and other layout decisions will ultimately shape when a line of talk and interaction ends. More importantly, definitions of utterance are likely to be only partially relevant to how interactants manage spoken communication. Therefore, a researcher must weigh the benefits of creating a transcript that reflects a theoretically informed definition of utterance, with the representational drawbacks of using a definition of utterance that imposes a system of speaking that is alien to the interactants under investigation.

3.3.4 Spacing

Another important organizational issue to take into consideration is spacing. Two spacing issues are particularly helpful when preparing documents for transcription work. The first issue is indentions, and the second issue is line spacing (e.g., single space versus double space).

Indentions are the white spaces located between line numbers, speakers, and rows of talk and interaction. As with line breaks, indentions should be set so that a transcript has relatively large white spaces. For instance, the following example has very little white space between each column of information, and thus results in a muddled, difficult-to-read, and unprofessional-looking transcript.

```
(13)   161   Merchant: =i- i remember not twenty five
       162   Peter: (was it) (1.0) °how much was it°
       163   (0.5)
       164   Merchant: fifty
       165   Peter: no it was forty
       166   Merchant: fifty
       167   Peter: it was fo:::::rty. yea:::h you
```

The example below, conversely, has relatively large white spaces. Consequently, the transcript is easier to read, and provides enough space to write analytic notes, if necessary.

```
(14)  161   Merchant:         =i- i remember not twenty five
      162   Peter:            (was it) (1.0) °how much was it°
      163                     (0.5)
      164   Merchant:         fifty
      165   Peter:            no it was forty
      166   Merchant:         fifty
      167   Peter:            it was fo::::rty. yea:::h you
```

Indentions are created by using the tab (tabulation) key or spacebar. While variation in tabulation presets may lead to portability issues when copying and pasting smaller segments of talk and interaction (cf. Extracts 11 and 12), the tab key is a much more efficient approach to creating indentions than the spacebar. Notwithstanding variation in tabulation presets, the tab key should only be used once or twice between each column of information. Too much white space will result in an unreadable transcript. In the example above, the tab key has been used once after the column of line numbers, and twice after the column of speakers. In addition to increasing readability, larger indentions provide the extra white necessary to highlight rows of talk and interaction that are noteworthy and analytically important. For example, arrows can be placed in white spaces in order to direct the reader to a particular phenomenon. For instance, the arrows in Extract 15 direct the reader to each instance of pause.

```
(15)  161   Merchant:         =i- i remember not twenty five
      162   Peter:      →     (was it) (1.0) °how much was it°
      163               →     (0.5)
      164   Merchant:         fifty
      165   Peter:            no it was forty
      166   Merchant:         fifty
      167   Peter:            it was fo::::rty. yea:::h you
```

The second issue is line spacing, and concerns the white space located between each row of talk and interaction. Specifically, line spacing refers to height of white space located from the bottom of one row to the top of the row below it. Unlike line breaks and indentions, line spacing has fewer implications with regard to the readability of transcripts. A general rule of thumb is to err on the side of creating large white spaces between each row of talk and interaction, as too little white space often results in a muddled transcript. Large white spaces between each row of talk and interaction allow researchers to circle and underline noteworthy features of communication, as well as make handwritten notes. Line spacing is typically set at 1.5 or 2.0 line spaces, or anything in between.

3.3.5 Placement of transcript

Transcripts are often broken into smaller segments of talk and interaction. These segments of talk and interaction are created because they allow researchers to easily share their analytic observations during conference presentations and/or for research publication (see Section 1.4). This section will discuss where segments of talk and interaction are placed in relation to written analyses (e.g., for the data analysis chapter of a doctoral dissertation). Segments of talk and interaction will generally include two supporting components of information: contextual overview and written analysis. The contextual overview introduces the interactants, communicative setting, and any other background information needed to assist the reader in understanding the analyzed segment. The contextual overview sets the scene, and helps establish an understanding of the larger transcript from which the segment has been taken. Consequently, the contextual overview is placed before the segment of talk and interaction.

The written analysis describes the segment, and provides observations that relate to an empirical aim, theme, and/or argument. More often than not, segments of talk and interaction are placed before written analyses. In so doing, the reader is given the opportunity to examine the segment – and generate her own observations – before reaching the written analysis. That is to say, the reader should be given the opportunity to examine the segment without being predisposed to a particular argument or observation. In terms of readability, it is also easier to follow the written analysis after the segment has been read and examined in detail.

3.4 Content

The last transcribing section in this chapter deals with the content of transcripts. The issues discussed below include what font type to use, how best to represent the interactants that have been recorded, and types of transcription detail. In other words, this section is concerned with the texts that make up transcripts. As with organizational issues, content issues play an important role in the readability, usability, and portability of transcripts.

3.4.1 Font type

Any given page of a transcript based on an audio recording of spoken interaction comprises approximately 80% text. Therefore, font type plays an important role in the representation of communication data. Despite the fact that there are numerous font types available in most word processing programs, only a few should be used for transcribing communication data. Two important points should be taken into consideration when selecting a font type. The first relates to the space that each character (letters, numbers, and symbols) occupies, and the second concerns the availability of symbols for paralinguistic representation (see also Section 3.4.3 and Chapter 4).

The space that each character occupies varies according to the type of font used. Font types fall into one of two 'spacing' categories. The first, and most common, is variable-width font. Example font types include Times New Roman (Font Example), Arial (Font Example), and Calibri (Font Example), to name a few. The space that is occupied with each character, and indeed the spacing between characters, varies, as the name suggests, with variable-width font. For example, with variable-width font (Times New Roman has been used below), the letter 'a' will occupy a different amount of space than, say, the number '9', as demonstrated in Extract 16.

(16) 1   Speaker A: a a a a a a a a a a
     2   Speaker B: 9 9 9 9 9 9 9 9 9 9

Now compare Extract 16 with the following example, which uses monospaced font (Courier New has been used below), the second spacing category.

(17) 1   Speaker A: a a a a a a a a a a
     2   Speaker B: 9 9 9 9 9 9 9 9 9 9

As illustrated in Extract 17, and as the name suggests, the characters of monospaced font occupy the same amount of space. Example font types include, but are not limited to, Courier New and Consolas. While the spacing differences between Extracts 16 and 17 appear minimal, the implications of using variable-width versus monospaced font are more significant when transcribing longer stretches of talk and interaction, where utterances are intertwined with intonational and turn management symbols. For example, instances of overlapping speech require carefully aligning two lines (rows) of talk with open '[' and close ']' brackets (see Chapter 4). As the following examples demonstrate, transcribing overlapping speech with monospaced font results in perfect alignment, thus promoting readability and usability (Extract 19), whereas the variable-width font (Extract 18), while not indecipherable, is unaligned and slightly unprofessional in appearance.

(18) 1   Speaker A: a a a a [a a a a] a a
     2   Speaker B: 9 9 9 9 [9 9 9 9] 9 9
(19) 1   Speaker A: a a a a [a a a a] a a
     2   Speaker B: 9 9 9 9 [9 9 9 9] 9 9

The second issue related to font selection is concerned with the characters and symbols used to transcribe paralinguistic features (e.g., abrupt stops, stress, intonation, and voice amplitude) and languages that do not use Roman alphabets. Transcribing paralinguistic features requires knowing that each font possesses a finite number of symbols. Unicode fonts, as in Lucida Sans Unicode and Arial Unicode MS, have a large selection of symbols that are used for transcribing paralinguistic features. Therefore, Unicode fonts should be used if the adopted notational system requires using a number of different symbols. A further benefit in using Unicode fonts is that they contain a large selection of characters, including non-Roman alphabets (e.g., Russian and Thai). Accordingly, Unicode fonts are particularly useful for transcribing multilingual data and languages that do not use Roman alphabets. With these issues in mind, Arial Unicode MS is an especially versatile font, as its large selection of characters and symbols is conducive for transcribing the paralinguistic features of many languages, while its monospaced setting allows for a more precise representation of overlapping talk.

3.4.2 Speaker representation

A small, but theoretically important, content issue concerns how interactants in data recordings are represented in transcripts. Two interrelated issues must be taken into consideration: labels and pseudonyms. First, a researcher must decide what labels best represent the interactants under investigation. If transcribing a stretch of talk between a doctor and patient, for example, then the interactants may be represented as 'doctor' and 'patient' or 'Joe' and 'Frank' or 'Speaker A' and 'Speaker B'. This decision should not be taken lightly, as labels influence how transcripts are read and interpreted. For instance, doctor and patient may suggest that the interactants are communicating and behaving in a particular way (i.e., like doctors and patients), and/or imply that there is an asymmetrical distribution of knowledge and power between both interactants. Indeed, these suggestions and implications are problematic if they are not relevant for the interactants and interaction. For example, the interactants could be talking about sports or politics, and this talk could occur outside the physical setting of the hospital. Therefore, as a transcript-based researcher, it is important to consider the social relevance and implications of labels, and to identify and problematize all possible labels available for the interactants and interaction under investigation. In other words, are the interactants demonstrably orienting to, for example, doctor and patient, and if not, would, say, Joe and Frank, better represent their talk and interaction?

The second issue regarding speaker representation is concerned with whether pseudonyms should be used to mask the identities of the interactants (see also Chapter 2). As circumstances pertaining to data collection and dissemination vary greatly from one institution to another, it is important to consult local policy regarding ethical procedures (for a discussion of data recording and transcribing ethics, see Rapley, 2007). It should be noted, however, that if confidentiality must be maintained, then the use of pseudonyms must not only be used for the names of the interactants, but also for place names, time and dates, and any other text in the transcript that reveals confidential information. Furthermore, as with the issue of labels discussed above, care should be taken when using pseudonyms, as they play an important role in how transcripts are read (for a review of approaches for using pseudonyms for people and place names, see Section 2.5).

3.4.3 Transcription detail

The last, but perhaps most important, content issue relates to how much detail is transcribed. In order to determine how much detail is needed, it is important to first identify what empirical purpose the transcript will serve. Will the transcript be used for presenting and publishing an analytic argument or a set of observations? If so, what methodology and methods will be used to analyze the data recording and transcripts? What social and interactional issues will be investigated? That is to say, transcription detail varies according to research interests and purposes. The decision to transcribe according to a particular level of detail will ultimately reflect the traditions of a research community and the methodology used to analyze the data recording and transcripts (see Chapter 2). While every attempt should be made to produce transcripts that closely resemble the data recording, it is also important to reemphasize (see Chapter 1) the fact that transcripts are approximations of real life events. That is to say, transcripts will never be able to fully capture all of the minute details of talk and interaction. This, on a conceptual level, is true, as transcripts are representations of past sayings and doings. On a practical level, transcripts are approximations of real life events, as the level of detail that can be provided is constrained by time, space, and technology. Researchers can only represent what is heard and seen in a data recording. A malfunctioning microphone will hinder a researcher's ability to represent the ways in which speech is delivered, the positioning of a recording device will influence what and how much nonverbal detail is represented, and using one video camera device to record several or more interactants communicating will insufficiently capture the complexities of multi-party talk and interaction, to name a few (for a more extended discussion of approaches to data recording, see Rapley, 2007).

Because the level of detail provided in a transcript is influenced and constrained by a number of different issues and variables, it is counterintuitive to prescribe a set of general guidelines that define what is an adequate level of transcription detail (for a discussion of a hierarchy of transcription detail, see Du Bois, 2006).

Therefore, the following table – which presents five types of transcription detail – should only be used as a starting point to determine what types of detail can be transcribed. For further clarification regarding what is acceptable transcription detail, it is useful to examine what other researchers working in the same investigatory area include in their published transcripts, and explore how levels and types of transcription detail correspond to different research questions/aims.

It is important to note that Table 3.2 should not be read linearly, from top to bottom. Transcripts with multimodal features will not necessarily include stress and intonation, while the omission of interactional features does not mean a transcript cannot include paralinguistic features. For instance, an investigation of hand gestures requires extensive Type 4 detail, but may not necessitate the same amount of Type 3 detail.

Because research traditions and aims determine how much detail (or granularity) will be included in a transcript, the next chapter will introduce and discuss three transcription systems that sufficiently cover Types 3 and 4 detail (i.e., interactional and paralinguistic). It should be noted again, however, that choosing a particular transcription system, and selecting which features of talk and interaction will be transcribed, requires understanding why and how the transcript will be used to carry out research. With that said, however, time and resources permitting, it is advisable to provide more transcription detail than is necessary for an analytic aim. Providing more transcription detail than is typically required of an analytic aim may turn out to be beneficial in that the extra level of detail may provide unforeseen empirical insights and direction (ten Have, 2002).

Table 3.2 Five Types of Transcription Detail

Type 1	*narrative*	i.e., a narrative account of the communicative event
Type 2	*orthographic*	i.e., words only
Type 3	*interactional*	e.g., pauses and overlapping speech
Type 4	*paralinguistic*	e.g., elongation, voice amplitude, stress, intonation
Type 5	*multimodal*	e.g., written notes and video stills of gestures

CHAPTER 4

Transcribing interactional and paralinguistic features

4.1 Introduction

The basic representational issues discussed in Chapter 3 are important in determining which media playback software program to use, how much white space to include in the margins, and what font type and size to use for transcribing, to name a few. While addressing basic representational issues is a necessary and crucial part of producing transcripts, transcribing requires a great deal of time and effort spent on representing interactional and paralinguistic features. Interactional features include, but are not limited to, overlapping talk, turn-taking, and pauses. Paralanguage includes any voice quality and pattern added to speech that bring meaning to words and utterances, and include, but are not limited to, elongation, stress, intonation, and voice amplitude.

While levels of granularity are dependent on research aims and intended audience (see Chapter 2), it is good practice – time and resources permitting – to include enough transcription detail to bare some resemblance to the data recording. Minimally, this would include carefully timed pauses, turn-taking transitions (e.g., overlapping and contiguous talk), and some paralinguistic features. Transcripts devoid of these interactional and paralinguistic features provide little in the way of illustrating to readers the precision and skilfulness in which talk and interaction is managed and used to carry out social actions.

The aim of this chapter is to identify and discuss the interactional and paralinguistic features that are commonly transcribed in the social and human sciences. The discussions contained in this chapter will equip readers with the necessary skills and knowledge to add depth and richness to their transcripts. The chapter is divided into two sections: interactional and paralinguistic features. Each section comprises three aims: (1) to provide a short, but detailed review of the reasons why the features in question should be transcribed, with references to relevant studies, (2) to discuss – using sample extracts – what notation symbols are used to transcribe interactional and paralinguistic features, and (3) to explain how transcription conventions are used.

Transcribing interactional and paralinguistic features requires using a transcription system. Transcription systems comprise conventions for representing talk and interaction. In most transcription systems, the standard convention for representing talk and interaction is to use symbols and punctuation markers. For each unique interactional and paralinguistic feature, there is generally a symbol or punctuation marker used to represent it in transcripts. In this chapter, three commonly used transcription systems are discussed.

4.2 Transcription conventions

The three transcription systems reviewed in this chapter are: conversation analysis (CA; see Jefferson, 2004), Santa Barbara School (SBS; see Du Bois, Schuetze-Coburn, Cumming, & Paolino, 1993), and Gesprächsanalytisches Transkriptionssystem 2 (GAT 2; see Selting, Auer, Barth-Weingarten, Bergmann, Bergmann, Birkner, Couper-Kuhlen, Deppermann, Gilles, Günthner, Hartung, Kern, Mertzlufft, Meyer, Morek, Oberzaucher, Peters, Quasthoff, Schütte, Stukenbrock, Uhmann, 2009; for GAT 1, see Selting, Auer, Barden, Bergmann, Couper-Kuhlen, Gunthner, Meier, Quasthoff, Schlobinski, & Uhmann, 1998). In the interest of simplicity, GAT 2 will be referred to as GAT.

The reason for reviewing three transcription systems – as opposed to, say, four or five – is two-fold. First, while other transcription systems exist, many are not widely used (cf. 'Transcription Notation', see Gumperz & Berenz, 1993). Conversely, CA, SBS, and GAT are all widely used for research dissemination and publication. Second, the three transcription systems reviewed here are relatively easy to apply in that they require little background reading regarding how each symbol or punctuation marker is used to represent talk and interaction. Conversely, some transcription systems – most notably 'Codes for the human analysis of transcripts' (CHAT) – require extensive background reading before transcribing can be done (see MacWhinney, 1995). It is hoped that the decision to review three widely-used, but accessible transcription systems will enhance the comprehensibility of the chapter, and provide the information necessary to make informed decisions regarding which convention to use and/or adapt (for an abridged overview of the three transcription systems discussed in this chapter, see Appendix C). Before identifying the conventions used to transcribe interactional and paralinguistic features, a brief overview for each system will be provided.

CA transcription conventions were established and developed by Gail Jefferson over three decades ago (see Atkinson & Heritage, 1984), in response to an emergent interest in sociology to examine talk and interaction in its own right. At the time, conversation analysts – for example, Harvey Sacks, Gail Jefferson, and Emanuel Schegloff – were concerned with understanding the mundane and micro aspects talk and interaction. This interest was predicated on the notion that researching how interactants precisely project speakership, use intonation to manage turn-taking, and time pauses to deal with overlapping talk, to name a few, can only be done with a transcript that is highly detailed in the ways in which interaction is conducted and speech is delivered. Consequently, CA's interest in the details of talk and interaction led to a set of transcription conventions that are now widely used for transcript-based research.

SBS conventions are associated with the work of John W. Du Bois and colleagues, though earlier incarnations existed under the name discourse transcription (DT) conventions (Du Bois et al., 1993). As with CA, SBS conventions have been created for the primary purpose of analyzing spoken interaction. The SBS transcription system consists of symbols and punctuation markers that are similar to those used in the CA transcription system, though – as demonstrated below – some differences exist. The Santa Barbara Corpus of Spoken American English is an example of a substantial collection of data that has been transcribed using SBS conventions (see Du Bois, Chafe, Meyer, & Thompson, 2000).

GAT conventions are also made up of symbols and punctuation markers that are used for representing and analyzing the micro details of spoken interaction. The GAT transcription system is an offshoot of the conventions used in CA, with some additional symbols and punctuation markers used for the analysis of prosody (see below). GAT is used primarily in Continental Europe, and in particular Germany (Selting et al., 1998). A ten-year anniversary of GAT has led to minor changes and a revised second edition (see Selting et al., 2009).

It is now prudent to provide a few provisos regarding the review of transcription systems that follows. The discussion of interactional and paralinguistic features below do not comprehensively review all conventions used for each transcription system, though the conventions that are discussed represent the most commonly used. When necessary, references to further reading will be provided. Furthermore, because transcription systems evolve over time to address unique disciplinary interests and research objectives, the conventions identified and discussed below may deviate from earlier versions. When possible, references to different notation symbols will be provided. Finally, transcribing communication data requires extensive hands-on experience and practice, particularly in training the ear to hear and distinguish sound differences, fluctuations, and patterns. For instance, only time in front of a computer, listening to and transcribing data recordings, will provide the skills and experience necessary to distinguish a rise in intonation from a slight fall in intonation. Therefore, a reading of this chapter should be supplemented with time in front of a computer transcribing communication data. In other words, transcribing interactional and paralinguistic features not only requires knowing what convention to use, but also associating the sounds heard in a data recording with the appropriate transcription symbol or punctuation marker.

4.3 Interactional features

Spoken communication entails a series of reciprocal, sequentially unfolding utterances and actions between speaker and listener. Minimally, spoken communication comprises two mutually dependent processes: talk and interaction. For this section, the topic of discussion is related to the latter. That is, the transcription conventions discussed below capture how interactants manage their turns-at-talk, where pauses are situated as utterances unfold in interaction, and how utterances latch on to each other. The section is divided into two sections: turn-taking and pauses.

4.3.1 Turn-taking

Social actions and activities – for example, rejecting a business offer and teaching a foreign language – are organized by turns; turns that consist of words, audible sounds, or gestures, to name a few. Within and across these turns, requests are made, discussions are carried out, activities are organized and accomplished, and information is exchanged. Sacks, Schegloff, and Jefferson (1974, p. 696), state "… the presence of 'turns' [in spoken interaction] suggests an economy, with turns for something being valued – and with means for allocating them, which affect their relative distribution, as in economies." In other words, turns are not simply carriers of information, devoid of social meaning. Turns and turn-taking underpin all things social.

The three turn-taking phenomena typically captured in transcripts are: simultaneous, overlapping, and contiguous utterances.

4.3.1.1 *Simultaneous utterances*

Simultaneous utterances occur when two or more interactants begin speaking at the same time, usually after a pause. With CA and SBS conventions, there are two notation symbols used to capture simultaneous talk. For the onset of simultaneous talk, double open brackets are used '[['. For the terminal point, double close brackets are used ']]'. GAT conventions – and some adaptations of the CA transcription system – use single open '[' and close brackets ']' for simultaneous utterances, the same notation symbols used for overlapping utterances (see Section 4.3.1.2). In Extract 1, the simultaneous talk that occurs between Peter and the Merchant is transcribed using double brackets.

```
(1)  84  Peter:     no (.) that's not fair (.) so::
         85                well it's fair for me but not
         86                fair for you
         87                (3.0)
```

```
    88   Peter:       [[so what's your price]]
    89   Merchant:    [[i'll give you a good]] price
```

In lines 88 and 89, the onset of simultaneous talk occurs at the beginning of both interactants' turns, as the double open brackets indicate. The termination of simultaneous talk occurs at the end of Peter's turn, and before the last word spoken by the merchant. In this example, the two turns begin with simultaneous talk, but end at different points. Therefore, it is useful to think and speak of simultaneous utterances as having onset and terminal points. Transcribing terminal points is useful because 'complete' simultaneous utterances – where two or more utterances begin and end at the same time – do not occur often. Furthermore, to enhance the readability of transcripts, it is generally good transcription practice to include both onset and terminal points. Transcripts with onset and terminal points marked are especially beneficial for analyzing multi-party interaction, where simultaneous, overlapping, and contiguous utterances, are the norm. Transcribing onset and terminal points in simultaneous talk makes it easier for readers to follow the flow of interaction, from one speaker to another.

4.3.1.2 *Overlapping utterances*

Overlapping utterances occur when one or more interactants speak or say something during another turn at talk. With all three transcription systems, the notation symbols used for overlapping utterances are similar to the conventions used for simultaneous utterances. The only difference is that in overlapping utterances, single brackets are used. Specifically, a single open bracket is used to represent the onset of overlapping talk '[', and a single close bracket ']' is used for terminal points. In Extract 2, overlapping utterances occur in lines 16 and 17.

```
(2)  14   Chris:       you↓ don't↑ remember him?
     15                (1.2)
     16   Peter:       no:::, we're a[ll
     17   Merchant:                  [i remember you
```

Note that in lines 16 and 17, there are no close brackets to denote the termination of overlapping talk. This is because the overlapping utterances terminate at the end of the turn, with no talk immediately following either utterance. The decision to exclude close brackets in these instances is a matter of personal choice and style. The omission of close brackets here does not hinder the readability of the transcript. However, when overlapping utterances are immediately followed by a turn spoken by a different interactant, close brackets assist readers in following the flow of interaction. For instance, in Extract 3, Peter continues speaking after his turn interjection in line 236.

(3) 235   Merchant: =na↓ha↑[haha i'm sorry]
    236   Peter: [it's okay   ] alright
    237   no problem thanks very mu[ch

The close bracket in line 236 marks the point where Peter continues with his talk immediately after the termination of overlapping talk, providing more context-sensitive information regarding who said what and when. It should be noted that the extra white space inside the brackets of Peter's overlapping talk indicates that Peter continues to talk in overlap until the end of the Merchant's previous turn. Alternatively, this phenomenon can be represented by stretching the overlapping talk to fit the entire width of the brackets: '[i t' s o k a y]'. It should also be noted that 'alright' is transcribed on the same line as Peter's overlapping utterance. This decision is based on the idea that placing 'alright' after the termination of overlapping talk better captures turn transitions. However, it is not uncommon to begin a new line when transcribing the talk that occurs after overlapping utterances (see Extract 4).

(4) 235   Merchant: =na↓ha↑[haha i'm sorry]
    236   Peter: [it's okay   ]
    237   alright no problem
    238   thanks very mu[ch

For many researchers, the decision to transcribe the continuation of talk on a new line is influenced, in part, by the belief that each line of talk should represent one complete utterance. Again, while adopting this approach may provide a more systematic way of representing talk that occurs after overlapping utterances, many researchers find it difficult to identify a definition of utterance that does not impose a system of speaking that is alien to the interactants under investigation. Furthermore, many researchers find that the practicalities of transcribing data recordings dictate when to end a line of talk. For example, it is not uncommon for researchers to end a line of talk because of margin sizes (see Section 3.3).

Typically, utterances that form overlapping talk are aligned and transcribed on separate lines (cf. Extract 3). Again, the main reason for doing so is to enhance the readability of transcripts. However, utterances that form overlapping talk often occupy more than one transcription line. For instance, in Extract 5, Peter's overlapping utterance occupies two lines of talk, whereas the Merchant's overlapping utterance occupies only one line.

(5) 136   Merchant: yeah i[f this one broken you-]
    137   Peter: [otherwise i would have to
    138   come back to china] and bring-=
    139   Merchant: =yes

Longer stretches of overlapping talk require breaking up utterances into different lines, thus necessitating the need to transcribe onset and terminal points. Although the terminal point will not be aligned in longer stretches of overlapping talk (see lines 136 and 138), the reader will be able to use the onset point to determine how the overlapping talk unfolds (see lines 136 and 137).

With SBS, instances of overlapping talk are numbered when they occur more than once in an exchange, further enhancing the readability of transcripts, as well as an understanding of when and where overlapping utterances occur.

```
(6)   77   Chris:      =he[₁he
      78   Merchant:      [₁ha↑hahaha↑  ·h[₂hh
      79   Peter:                          [₂that's i
```

The practice of numbering overlapping utterances is also beneficial when analyzing and disseminating data, as researchers can refer to specific instances of talk in a more efficient manner.

4.3.1.3 *Contiguous utterances*

Contiguous utterances occur when one sound, word, or utterance is followed by another sound, word, or utterance. Generally speaking, spoken interaction is a series of contiguous utterances. However, in transcription terms, the convention for transcribing contiguous utterances is used specifically for two representational purposes: the latching of two lines of talk spoken by two different speakers and the latching of two lines of talk spoken by the same speaker. All three transcription systems use the same notation symbol for latching. That is, the notation symbol used for latching is the equal sign '='. The first type of latching occurs when one speaker turn is immediately followed by another speaker turn spoken by a different interactant. In Extract 7, this type of latching occurs in lines 138 and 139.

```
(7)   137   Peter:         [otherwise i would have to
      138                  come back to china] and bring-=
      139   Merchant:    =yes
      140   Peter:       and come and see you
```

In more complex, multi-party exchanges, latching occurs in conjunction with overlapping utterances. In Extract 8, for example, Peter and the Merchant engage in overlapping talk (lines 21 and 22), while Chris' utterance in line 23 latches on to the end of Peter's utterance in line 21.

```
(8)   20   Chris:      do you remember he bought=
      21   Peter:      =he['s young and hands[ome=
      22   Merchant:      [hehe              [no no no
      23   Chris:      =he-
```

In complex exchanges like this, a researcher must decide what two lines of talk – out of the series of overlapping and latching utterances – will be adjacently placed. For example, in lines 21 and 23, the latching of talk is displaced with the Merchant's overlapping talk (compare this with Extract 7). The Merchant's talk is located directly under Peter's turn because transcripts are generally easier to read when overlapping utterances are adjacently placed (cf. Extract 3). When overlapping utterances are separated, as in Extract 9, it is more difficult to follow who engages in overlapping talk, and at what points the overlapping talk begins and ends.

```
(9)  20  Chris:      do you remember he bought=
     21  Peter:      =he['s young and hands[ome=
     22  Chris:      =he-
     23  Merchant:        [hehe           [no no no
```

The convention for contiguous utterances is also used to represent the latching of two lines of talk spoken by the same interactant. To illustrate this type of contiguity, Extract 8 has been slightly modified and reproduced as Extract 10.

```
(10) 21  Peter:      he['s young and handsome=
     22  Merchant:      [hehe
     23  Peter:      =he's young and handsome
```

Peter's utterances are represented in two displaced lines of talk in order to show that his turn continues as the Merchant interjects with laughter. Representing latching of this type is often necessary when a turn spans several lines of talk while other interactants are speaking and/or interacting.

4.3.2 Pauses

Despite the omnipresence of pauses in spoken communication, it is not uncommon to see pauses transcribed with subjective approximations. Indeed, some researchers do not transcribe pauses at all. However, as with turn-taking, pauses are not devoid of social meaning. Studies have shown that interactants use pauses to deal with overlapping talk in online settings where people can hear but not see each other (Jenks, 2009), display a preference or orientation to a previous turn, for example when declining an offer or invitation (Hutchby & Wooffitt, 2008), and manage gaze and turn-taking practices (Goodwin, 1980). The length of pauses has also been shown to play an important role in the prosodic quality of surrounding talk (Krivokapić, 2007). In short, pauses are an important part of spoken communication. Fortunately, the task of timing pauses has been made easier with advances in software technology. Many freely available media playback programs allow users to quickly and precisely time pauses (see Chapter 3), so researchers should not overlook them during the transcription process.

Two pause phenomena will be discussed in this section: timed and micro pauses.

4.3.2.1 *Timed pauses*

With CA pauses are timed when they last longer than one tenth of a second (or approximately two tenths of a second and fifteen hundredths of a second for GAT and SBS, respectively). All three transcription systems use the same notation symbol for timed pauses. Timed pauses are represented numerically inside a single set of parentheses. For example, six tenths of a second is represented as (0.6), as in Extract 11, line 37.

```
(11)  36 Peter:      remember me
      37             (0.6)
      38 Merchant:   no I'm j[ust (joke) you
```

Some researchers represent pauses with two or more decimal points (e.g., one hundredth of a second or more), in order to provide a greater level of transcription detail, though it is not common practice to do so. Timed pauses are placed either within the same line of talk or on a separate line. In line 37, the timed pause is placed on a separate line because it occurs between two interactants. Placing pauses on a separate line between two interactants is helpful in showing when turn transitions occur. A timed pause is also placed on a separate line between two turns spoken by the same interactant when it is necessary to show that the pause represents a transition relevant place (for an example, see Appendix A, lines 84–88).

For longer turns spoken by the same interactant, timed pauses are placed within the same line, as in Extract 12, line 68.

```
(12)  68 Peter:      if you don't mind (1.0)
      69             a:nd, what's the price for them
      70             (1.0)
      71 Merchant:   how much you want?
```

Here the timed pause is located within Peter's turn. This approach allows researchers to show that the interactant holds the conversational floor during the pause.

The examples discussed in this section show that the placement of timed pauses has implications for how a transcript is read. While it is not necessary to transcribe every instance of pause, researchers must be mindful of the fact that pauses perform many different social-interactional functions.

4.3.2.2 *Micro pauses*

CA and GAT use the same notation symbol for transcribing micro pauses. However, CA and GAT differ in terms of what constitutes a micro pause. With CA, a micro pause is approximately one tenth of a second or less. With GAT, a micro pause is precisely two tenths of a second. The notation symbol used to represent micro pauses is a period/full stop inside a single set of parentheses. For example, in Extract 13, the micro pause occurs in line 60.

```
(13)  59 Peter:      ooops ((bumps into merchandise))
      60             (.)
      61 Merchant:   that's okay hehehe [sorry
```

With SBS, micro pauses are represented as either two or three periods/full stops, depending on approximately how long the pauses are. A short micro pause, which is represented as two periods/full stops, is approximately less than fifteen hundredths of a second, whereas a long micro pause, which is represented as three periods/full stops, is approximately more than fifteen hundredths of a second. In Extract 14, a short micro pause has been transcribed using the SBS notation symbol.

```
(14)  59 Peter:      ooops ((bumps into merchandise))
      60             ..
      61 Merchant:   that's okay hehehe [sorry
```

All three transcription systems provide a somewhat reliable and accurate way of representing micro pauses. Stylistically, SBS may adopt the most appropriate notation symbol, given transcripts are largely text-based, and ellipses are often used in writing. However, some readers may confuse ellipses as omissions of talk, so researchers should explicitly describe the convention used. With CA and GAT, the practice of representing all pauses (both timed and micro) within a single set of parentheses provides a more systematic way of representing pauses. As with any transcription decision, personal preference and research needs should be factored in while deciding what convention and notation symbol to use.

4.4 Paralinguistic features

The paralinguistic (e.g., abrupt stops and elongations) and prosodic (e.g., stress and intonation) features of spoken communication accomplish many things (see Couper-Kuhlen, 2000). It allows interactants to string together words and utterances, creating meaning and understanding. Paralanguage, in particular prosody, follows a system of rule and structures, and without these rules and structures, meaning and understanding are potentially lost. Interactants use paralanguage as social-interactional resources, to help organize events and activities, establish familiarity and rapport, carry out communicative tasks, and so forth. Paralanguage is also used in subtler, but equally systematic ways. For instance, a slight fall in intonation at the end of an utterance can signal the end of a turn (Schegloff, 1998), or changes in accentuation can project an emotional stance (Goodwin & Goodwin, 2000). Because paralanguage does many things in spoken communication, transcribing stress and intonation, among other features, is helpful – perhaps even crucial – in doing transcript-based research.

However, paralanguage is omnipresent in spoken communication, so researchers must be selective in what to transcribe. Too much detail will hinder the readability of a transcript, while too little detail will reduce the ability to make analytic observations. Time and resources will often play a large part in how much detail is transcribed. The decision to transcribe at a particular level of granularity must also reflect personal and empirical concerns and interests (see Chapter 2). Perhaps more importantly, determining the most appropriate level of detail requires knowing why the paralinguistic feature(s) in question must be transcribed. In other words, what empirical purpose does the transcribed feature serve?

Transcribing the nuances of spoken communication not only requires a tremendous amount of time and effort, but also skill and experience. It takes many hours of experience listening to, and transcribing data recordings, to develop the skill necessary to distinguish between, for example, a rise and fall in intonation. While this skill is acquired largely through practical transcription experience with data recordings, researchers must also be familiar with the different notation symbols used for representing paralanguage. The aim of this section is to address this need. Although the discussions contained in this section do not comprehensively review every feature that can be transcribed, the conventions and symbols that are identified provide enough background information to produce highly detailed transcripts of talk and interaction.

This section is broken into seven subsections: intonation, elongation and abrupt stops, stress and voice amplitude, audible aspirations and inhalations, tempo, other voice qualities, and unintelligible speech (nb. unintelligible speech is neither paralinguistic nor prosodic, but included in this section because it is related to transcribing words and utterances).

4.4.1 Intonation

Much work has been done on how intonation is used in interaction (e.g., Couper-Kuhlen, 2000). Topics of investigation include, but are not limited to, how intonation is used to project speakership, elicit a response, interject and interrupt, request for clarification, complete each other's turns, and signal listenership. Intonation not only facilitates in the management of turn-taking practices, but also 'colors' a story or joke (Wade & Moore, 1986), helps establish affiliation (Hellermann, 2003), and displays politeness (Ofuka, McKeown, Waterman, & Roach, 2000). Studies that investigate how intonation is used in interaction vividly show that meaning and action are inextricably tied to the production of prosody.

The four intonation phenomena discussed in this section are: falling intonation, slight rising intonation, rising intonation, and marked upsteps/downsteps in intonation. The notation symbols reviewed here are from the CA transcription system. GAT and SBS use CA notation symbols, though small differences exist. When necessary, these differences will be identified and discussed.

4.4.1.1 *Falling intonation*

Falling intonation is a fall in pitch that occurs at the end of an utterance. This prosodic feature is generally transcribed when it occurs at the end of an utterance. Falls in intonation that occur within utterances are often not transcribed because they are difficult to hear without specialized software (only marked downsteps in intonation within utterances are typically transcribed; see Section 4.4.1.4). A fall in intonation that occurs at the end of an utterance is sometimes referred to as 'closing intonation', as this prosodic feature can signal the end of a turn. Falling intonation is represented in transcripts as a period/full stop '.'. As with all punctuation markers used as notation symbols, the period/full stop does not necessarily denote the end of a sentence. In Extract 15, line 45, the merchant delivers 'small' with falling intonation.

```
(15)  43  Peter:      it looks like i'll get him that
      44              one (3.0) it's too small
      45  Merchant:   too small. you↑ want↓ bigger↑
      46  Peter:      i think so
```

The delivery of falling intonation in this example demonstrates the importance of capturing prosodic features. Note that the period/full stop following 'too small' shows that the merchant in line 45 is acknowledging Peter's assessment of the size of the shirt, and is not challenging and/or questioning his assessment; the latter action is generally accomplished with rising intonation (see Sections 4.4.1.3 and 4.4.1.4). In CA terms, the fall in intonation also represents a potential opportunity for Peter to take a turn at talk (Sacks et al., 1974).

4.4.1.2 *Slight rising intonation*

Slight rising intonation is a small rise in pitch that is generally transcribed when it occurs at the end of an utterance. Slight rises in intonation that occur within utterances are not generally transcribed because they are difficult to hear without specialized software (only marked upsteps in intonation within utterances are typically transcribed; see Section 4.4.1.4). A slight rise in intonation that occurs at the end of an utterance is sometimes referred to as 'continuing intonation', as it generally signals that more talk is forthcoming. Slight rising intonation is represented as a comma ','. In Extract 16, slight rising intonation occurs in line 49, at the end of 'smal'.

```
(16)  45  Merchant:   too small. you↑ want↓ bigger↑
      46  Peter:      i think so
      47  Merchant:   okay
      48  Peter:      i think so
      49  Merchant:   yeh smal, i'll choos a large one
      50                  (4.0)
```

For stylistic and readability reasons, some researchers use commas as punctuation markers. Although it is not uncommon to see commas being used to mark boundaries between clauses, it is recommended that the use of commas is restricted to representing slight falls in intonation, as transcripts of communication data are fundamentally about capturing the way people talk and interact.

4.4.1.3 *Rising intonation*

Rising intonation is an inflected rise in pitch occurring at the end of an utterance, which is often – but not always – delivered as a question. Rising intonation, which is represented in transcripts as a question mark '?', is different than slight rising intonation (',') in that the former is more audibly significant. In Extract 17, Peter completes his turn in line 101 with rising intonation.

```
(17)  99   Merchant:  yeah i don't remember but i know
      100             not twenty
      101  Peter:     you su[re?
      102  Merchant:       [it was twenty (.) sure
      103             one hundred percent sure
```

With SBS, rising intonation is transcribed with a question mark, followed by a period/full stop '?.'. With some adaptations of CA, an inverted question mark '¿' is used to denote an audibly less significant rise in intonation. If inverted question marks are used in addition to question marks, then it is important to distinguish somewhere in the presentation of a transcript how the two notation symbols are used systematically (e.g., distinguishing the prosodic differences between more and less significant intonation rises).

4.4.1.4 *Marked upsteps/downsteps in intonation*

Marked upsteps and downsteps in intonation can occur in word/utterance initial, medial, and final positions, and they are often transcribed to denote a change or jump in intonation direction – from a rise to a fall, for example. A marked upstep in intonation is shorter in duration than rising intonation ('?'). For many researchers, the prosodic difference between a marked upstep in intonation and rising intonation does not warrant discrimination when transcribing. Indeed, the only way to systematically measure the prosodic difference between a marked upstep in intonation and rising intonation is to use specialized software. Because the prosodic difference between a marked upstep in intonation and rising intonation is ostensibly negligible, it is not uncommon to see researchers use one notation symbol for both types of intonation. If it is necessary to discriminate between the two prosodic features, then one solution is to transcribe marked upsteps in intonation only when they occur with marked downsteps in intonation (as well as transcribing downsteps in intonation only when they occur with upsteps in intonation), and rises in intonation when they occur at the end of utterances, and with no other immediately preceding marked change in intonation direction. Indeed, stylistically, the notation symbol used for rising intonation ('?') is better placed at the end of an utterance.

With CA and GAT, a marked upstep in intonation is represented as an upward arrow '↑', and a marked downstep in intonation is represented as a downward arrow '↓' (nb. the model transcript in Appendix A only uses arrows when they occur before or after a marked change in intonation direction). With GAT, larger upsteps and downsteps in intonation are represented as double upward '↑↑' and downward arrows '↓↓', respectively. With most adaptations of CA, the notation symbols used for marked upstepped/downstepped intonation are placed before the syllable that has the rise or fall in intonation. Some researchers, however, place the arrows after the rise or fall in intonation, as in Extract 18.

```
(18)   43   Peter:      it looks like i'll get him that
       44               one (3.0) it's too small
       45   Merchant:   too small. you↑ want↓ bigger↑
       46   Peter:      i think so
```

In line 45, the merchant delivers each word in the 'you want bigger' construction in three successive changing intonation directions. First, 'you' is delivered with an initial step up in intonation, and then 'want' with a final step down in intonation, and finally 'bigger' with a final step up in intonation. Again, a question mark is not used for the word 'bigger', as the intonation direction occurs after a marked downstep in intonation. Stylistically, the three arrows also provide a better visual representation of the three successive changes in intonation direction than a combination of two question marks and one downward arrow (cf. you? want↓ bigger?). Yet another approach to discriminating marked upsteps in intonation and rises in intonation is to only transcribe the former in utterance initial and medial positions, and the latter in utterance final positions (e.g., organi↑zation?).

As mentioned briefly above, some researchers place arrows before words and utterances (cf. '↑you ↓want ↑bigger'), though this approach is slightly less intuitive, as intonation occurs while syllables are uttered, not before. Indeed, the most appropriate way of representing different intonation patterns is to use notation symbols above utterances/syllables, though this approach is extremely time consuming without specialized software.

With SBS, the notation symbol '↑' is used in lieu of the upward arrow, while '↓' replaces the downward arrow.

4.4.2 Elongations and abrupt stops

Spoken communication is often fraught with hesitation, restarts, audible fillers, word lengthening, and other speech disfluencies. Sometimes these features of talk are investigated as representations of the inner workings of the brain (e.g., Levelt, 1983), while other researchers examine speech disfluencies in order to understand institutional workplace practices (e.g., Wilkinson, 2008). Two paralinguistic features that are often associated with speech disfluencies are elongations and abrupt stops. It is important to note, however, that elongations and abrupt stops are not only demonstrations of speech disfluencies. For example, the lengthening of a word can be used to maintain speakership, while an abrupt stop can serve to yield the conversational floor. Whatever social-interactional purpose they serve, elongations and abrupt stops are commonly heard in spoken communication. Fortunately, elongations and abrupt stops are less difficult to hear and transcribe than fluctuations in intonation patterns. CA, GAT, and SBS all use the same transcription conventions to represent elongations and abrupt stops.

4.4.2.1 *Elongations*

Elongations are extensions of sound that can occur anywhere during speech production (e.g., word medial and final positions). With CA, GAT, and SBS, elongated speech is represented as a colon ':', with more colons denoting longer stretches of sound. For instance, in Extract 19, line 92, the merchant produces an emphatic, elongated 'NO'.

```
(19)  90  Peter:      because last time you- you sold
      91              it for twenty (yuan)
      92  Merchant:   NO::::[::
      93  Peter:            [hehe
      94  Chris:            [hehe
      95  Peter:      you did.
```

If elongated speech is prevalent in a data recording, then it is recommended to adopt a system that allows for efficient and accurate representations of sound extensions. One way of accomplishing this is to place a time value, say one tenth of second, for each colon used. This approach would not only lead to faster and more accurately transcribed data, but it would also allow readers to determine the length of each elongated sound. For instance, the six colons in line 92 would represent elongation of six tenths of a second.

4.4.2.2 *Abrupt stops*

An abrupt stop is a cut-off in sound. With all three transcription systems, an abrupt stop is represented in transcripts as a hyphen '-'. With GAT, a glottal stop symbol is used in cases where the abrupt stop is achieved glottally ('?'). Abrupt stops can occur anywhere during talk, though they tend to occur during turn transitions. For example, in Extract 20, an abrupt stop in articulation occurs in line 28, immediately before Peter take his turn. The second abrupt stop occurs in line 29, immediately before the merchant overlaps with Peter's turn.

```
(20)  27  Peter:     and i'm just an ugly old fart
      28  Chris:     he ma-
      29  Peter:     i know i don't c- [that's okay]
      30  Merchant:                    [oh:::::     ]
```

Abrupt stops in articulation often occur before a restart, as is the case in Extract 21, line 75.

```
(21)  75  Peter:     [well i- if you're asking, i
      76             want you to give it to me=
```

Here Peter begins his turn ('well i-'), and then restarts with a new formulation ('if you're asking').

4.4.3 Stress and voice amplitude

Adjustments and fluctuations in stress and voice amplitude do many things in spoken communication (Couper-Kuhlen, 2000). For example, by stressing certain words or sounds of words, an interactant can forefront an interactionally salient issue (Selting, 1994). Increasing voice amplitude can serve to reinforce a decision or response, or in other situations, speaking loudly plays an important role in competing for the conversational floor during overlapping talk. Stress and voice amplitude – like all paralinguistic features – are used in distinctive ways, and vary in use from setting to setting, and indeed, moment by moment.

The three commonly transcribed stress and voice amplitude features are emphasis, loud/forte speech, and soft/piano speech. The notation symbols used for stress and voice amplitude are different each transcription system.

4.4.3.1 *Emphasis*

All spoken utterances are marked with some degree of prominence or accentuation. The placement of prominence or accentuation on certain syllables is, in part, what gives an utterance a unique meaning. While it is not necessary to transcribe accentuation in every utterance (this would be done only for special research purposes), it is feasible to transcribe accentuation when it is used for special social-interactional purposes, say to emphatically reject a proposal or to accept an invitation. It is more feasible to transcribe these types of emphatic prominence because, simply put, they occur less frequently and systematically than accent-related prominence.

With CA, the procedure for transcribing emphasis is to underline the accentuated word or sound. For example, in Extract 22, line 16, the merchant emphasizes the word 'you' (nb. words delivered with extra strong accent are capitalized and underlined).

```
(22)  71 Merchant:    how much you want?
      72               (0.5)
      73 Peter:       how much do i want=
```

With GAT, the same emphasized word is transcribed by capitalizing the word 'you' ('YOU'). If the word is delivered with extra strong accent, then two exclamation marks are placed on both sides of the emphasized word, as illustrated in Extract 23.

```
(23)  71 Merchant:    how much !YOU! want?
      72               (0.5)
      73 Peter:       how much do i want=
```

Finally, with SBS, the type of emphasis discussed above is referred to as primary accent. Primary accent is transcribed using the carrot notation symbol '^', and placed before the emphasized word.

```
(24)  71 Merchant:    how much ^you want
      72               (0.5)
      73 Peter:       how much do i want=
```

4.4.3.2 *Loud/forte speech*

With CA, utterances spoken louder than adjacent talk are represented with capital letters, as in Extract 25, line 92.

```
(25)  90 Peter:       because last time you- you sold
      91               it for twenty (yuan)
      92 Merchant:    NO::::[::
```

With GAT, the 'no' produced in line 92 is transcribed using a descriptor – in this case 'f' for forte – and is placed within a set of angled brackets (i.e., <f>). This descriptor is placed before the utterance that is spoken louder than adjacent talk. An outer set of angled brackets is then placed on both sides of the utterance that is spoken louder than adjacent talk. Therefore, with GAT, two sets of angled brackets are used. First, an inner set is used for the descriptor. Second, an outer set is used to capture the entire utterance (nb. the use of descriptors and angled brackets aids in the use of computer-assisted, corpus-driven analytic tools).

```
(26)  90  Peter:       because last time you- you sold
      91               it for twenty (yuan)
      92  Merchant:    <<f>NO::::[::>
```

GAT conventions also have a representational system for speech that becomes increasingly louder. In these situations, the abbreviation 'cresc' (crescendo) replaces the 'f': <<cresc>word>. SBS is similar to GAT, with only minor differences. Specifically, SBS uses a descriptor – in this case a capital 'F' – within a set of angled brackets. The descriptor is then placed before the utterance that is spoken louder than surrounding talk. A second descriptor is placed at the end of the utterance that is spoken louder than surrounding talk, this time with a forward slash '/'.

```
(27)  90  Peter:       because last time you- you sold
      91               it for twenty (yuan)
      92  Merchant:    <F>NO::::[::</F>
```

A benefit in using greater-than and less-than signs (i.e., angled brackets) as a representational system for paralinguistic features is that it allows researchers to easily code and locate particular instances of talk. However, a disadvantage in this system is that transcripts can appear muddled, and therefore difficult to read without computer-assisted tools.

4.4.3.3 *Soft/piano speech*

Words and utterances spoken softer than surrounding talk are represented by two symbols on both sides of the quiet speech. With CA, the notation symbol used is a 'degree' sign. In Extract 28, line 155, Peter utters the words 'one at forty' more softly than surrounding talk.

```
(28)  154  Peter:      [do i want anything else yeah
      155              (1.0) °one at forty° oh sorry
      156              [twenty five yeah
      157  Chris:      [how much are you paying for it?
```

With GAT, 'one at forty' is transcribed with the same convention used for representing loud/forte speech, though a 'p' is used as the descriptor.

```
(29)  154  Peter:      [do i want anything else yeah
      155              (1.0) <<p>one at forty> oh sorry
      156              [twenty five yeah
      157  Chris:      [how much are you paying for it?
```

GAT also has a convention for talk that becomes increasingly softer. In these situations, the abbreviation 'dim' (diminuendo) replaces the 'p': <<dim>word>. Finally, for soft/piano speech, SBS uses a convention that is similar to GAT.

```
(30)  154   Peter:     [do i want anything else yeah
      155              (1.0) <P>one at forty</P> oh
      156              sorry [twenty five yeah
      157   Chris:     [how much are you paying for it?
```

4.4.4 Audible aspirations and inhalations

While intonation, stress, and voice amplitude, are inextricably tied to meaning and action – and are thus the most commonly transcribe paralinguistic features of talk – audible aspirations and inhalations play an important role in talk and interaction. The sounds that come from audibly breathing in and out can assist in the management of turn-taking (Sacks et al., 1974), especially in communicative settings where interactants cannot see each other (Jenks, 2009). Laughter, a combination of audible aspirations and inhalations, has been investigated extensively and shown to be closely linked to the production of meaning. Research shows that laughter assists in terminating topics (Holt, 2010), reveals institutional asymmetries (Glenn, 2010), and displays interactional identities (Voge, 2010). Though laughter is notoriously difficult to transcribe (Jefferson, 1985), it is a feature of spoken communication that warrants careful representation (Potter & Hepburn, 2010).

Four features of audible aspirations and inhalations are reviewed: exhalations, laugh particle, laughter within a word, and inhalations.

4.4.4.1 *Exhalations*

Exhalations include any breathing out sound made before, during, and after a spoken utterance or laughter. With CA, audible exhalations that occur before or after a spoken utterance are represented with the letter 'h', with more letters denoting longer stretches of exhalation. In Extract 31, line 145, Peter exhales immediately before two laugh particles.

```
(31)  143   Peter:      very angry
      144   Merchant:   okay
      145   Peter:      eh hh[   ha ha   ]
      146   Merchant:        [no problem]
```

With GAT, the exhalation in line 145 is transcribed using the letter 'h' with a degree sign '°' to the right of the sound production.

```
(32)  143   Peter:      very angry
      144   Merchant:   okay
```

```
145  Peter:      eh hh°[  ha ha  ]
146  Merchant:         [no problem]
```

Finally, with SBS, exhalations are transcribed using a capital 'H' and lower case 'x' inside open and close parentheses. Unlike CA and GAT, longer stretches of exhalation are not represented with additional letters.

```
(33)  143  Peter:      very angry
      144  Merchant:   okay
      145  Peter:      eh (Hx)[  ha ha  ]
      146  Merchant:          [no problem]
```

4.4.4.2 *Laugh particle*

A laugh particle is a single sound unit that often forms longer stretches of laughter. Although the sounds produced during laughter vary greatly, the most commonly heard and transcribed laugh particles are 'he' and 'ha'. With CA and GAT, these laugh particles are used to transcribe laughter. In Extract 34, line 19, the merchant produced three 'he' laugh particles.

```
(34)  16  Peter:      no:::, we're a[ll
      17  Merchant:                  [i remember you
      18  Chris:      o:kay=
      19  Merchant:   =hehehe
```

With SBS, laugh particles are transcribed using the 'at' symbol. For each laugh particle produced, an 'at' symbol is used.

```
(35)  16  Peter:      no:::, we're a[ll
      17  Merchant:                  [i remember you
      18  Chris:      o:kay=
      19  Merchant:   =@ @ @
```

4.4.4.3 *Laughter within an utterance*

With CA, laughter produced within an utterance is transcribed using laugh particles – or audible aspiration or inhalation particles – within open and close parentheses. For example, in Extract 36, line 123, the merchant produces three laugh particles within/between the production of two words. Although strictly speaking 'other' and 'store' are two words, they are delivered within a single stretch of talk with no break in sound occurring at the beginning and end points of laughter. That is to say, any laughter occurring within an utterance or adjacent to other talk, with no break in sound, should be transcribed using laugh particles within parentheses.

```
(36)  121  Merchant:   no that's (g[o to)
      122  Chris:                  [ehhaha
      123  Merchant:   other(hehehe)store (h[elp you)
```

With GAT, laughter within or adjacent to an utterance is transcribed using greater-than and less-than signs, with the word 'laugh' embedded to the left of the laughter.

(37) 121 Merchant: no that's (g[o to)
     122 Chris: [ehhaha
     123 Merchant: other<<laugh>hehehe>store (h[elp

With SBS, the 'at' sign is used for each time a laugh particle is produced within or adjacent to an utterance.

(38) 121 Merchant: no that's (g[o to)
     122 Chris: [ehhaha
     123 Merchant: other@ @ @store (h[elp you)

4.4.4.4 Inhalations

Inhalations include any breathing in sound made before, during, and after a spoken utterance or laughter. With CA, audible inhalations that occur before or after a spoken utterance are represented with a period/full stop to the left of the letter 'h', with more letters denoting longer stretches of inhalation. In Extract 39, line 125, the merchant inhales immediately after three laugh particles.

(39) 125 Merchant: hehehehe.hh
     126   (1.0)
     127 Peter: so (yeah)=
     128 Merchant: =so

With GAT, the inhalation in line 125 is transcribed using the letter 'h' with a 'degree' sign to the left of the sound.

(40) 125 Merchant: hehehehe°hh
     126   (1.0)
     127 Peter: so (yeah)=
     128 Merchant: =so

With SBS, exhalations are transcribed using a capital 'H' inside open and close parentheses. Unlike CA and GAT, longer stretches of inhalation are not represented with additional letters.

(41) 125 Merchant: hehehehe (H)
     126   (1.0)
     127 Peter: so (yeah)=
     128 Merchant: =so

4.4.5 Tempo

The speeding up and slowing down of talk is often synchronized with the tempo of speech spoken by fellow interactants. The delicate synchronization of tempo is a means for co-constructing meaning and accomplishing social actions. Tempo is used for rhetorical purposes (Couper-Kuhlen, 1993), to display an emotional state (Selting, 1994), and as a resource for managing conversational floors (Auer, Couper-Kuhlen, & Muller, 1999), to name a few.

The two tempo-related features that are reviewed in this section are: faster/allegro and slower/lento talk. CA and GAT have different conventions for both features, while SBS does not have a convention for representing faster and slower talk.

4.4.5.1 *Faster/allegro talk*

With CA, talk spoken faster than adjacent utterances is transcribed using an 'arrow' on each side of the faster speech. Some researchers point both arrows in, to denote compression of the spoken words (e.g., >I am speaking faster<), while others point both arrows to the right, to denote a faster delivery. In Extract 42, line 26, for example, the merchant produces 'no' in two, quick successive instances following an elongated 'no'.

```
(42)   24  Peter:      he's young and handsome
       25  Chris:      no.
       26  Merchant:   no::: >no no>
```

With GAT, the faster talk produced in line 26 is transcribed using the abbreviation 'all' (allegro) with the same series of greater-than and less-than signs discussed previously.

```
(43)   24  Peter:      he's young and handsome
       25  Chris:      no.
       26  Merchant:   no::: <<all>no no>
```

GAT also has a convention for representing talk that becomes increasingly faster. In these instances, the abbreviation 'acc' (accelerando) is used.

4.4.5.2 *Slower/lento talk*

With CA, talk spoken slower than adjacent utterances is transcribed using an 'arrow' on each side of the slower speech. Some researchers point both arrows out, to denote elongation (e.g., <I am speaking slower>), while others point both arrows to the left, to denote a slower delivery. In Extract 44, line 10, for example, Peter produces 'we'll see' slower than adjacent talk.

```
(44)   10  Peter:      uh:: maybe. <we::ll see< >we'll
       11              see> what we can do
       12  Merchant:   o::kay. (.) no problem
```

With GAT, the slower talk produced in line 10 is transcribed using the abbreviation 'len' (lento) with greater-than and less-than signs.

(45) 10 Peter: uh:: maybe. <<len>we::ll see>
      11   >we'll see> what we can do
      12 Merchant: o::kay. (.) no problem

GAT also differentiates between slower talk and talk that becomes increasingly slower. For the latter, the abbreviation 'rall' (rallentando) is used.

4.4.6 Other voice qualities

The transcription conventions reviewed thus far are often enough to transcribe most of what is heard in data recordings. Occasionally, however, a paralinguistic feature heard in a data recording will not have a notation symbol. In these situations, it is common practice to create a new notation symbol and convention that represents the sound that must be transcribed (for a discussion of add-on conventions, see Section 6.3.5). These less frequently used notation symbols are often grouped under the heading 'other voice qualities'. The other voice quality discussed in this section is smile voice.

4.4.6.1 *Smile voice*

Smile voice is the auditory quality that talk has when it is uttered with a smile (Drahota, Costall, Reddy, 2008). Sometimes smile voice is produced around instances of laughter, though this is not always the case. With CA, smile voice is transcribed using two dollar signs '$', one on each side of the talk produced with a smile (nb. some researchers use the pound sterling sign '£'). In Extract 46, line 149, Peter produces a smile voice in overlap with the merchant's turn.

(46) 147 Peter: hahaha
      148 Merchant: you stronger th[an me no problem
      149 Peter: [$°no problem°$
      150 Merchant: yo[u don't a worry]

With GAT, smile voice is transcribed using a series of greater-than and less-than signs with an embedded smiley face emoticon.

(47) 147 Peter: hahaha
      148 Merchant: you stronger th[an me no problem
      149 Peter: [<<:-)>°no
      150   problem°>

SBS uses a different smiley face emoticon with a slightly different combination of greater-than and less-than signs.

68 Transcribing talk and interaction

(48) 147 Peter: hahaha
     148 Merchant: you stronger th[an me no problem
     149 Peter: [<☺>°no
     150   problem°</☺>

It should be noted that not all paralinguistic features require a unique notation symbol. Often a paralinguistic feature only occurs once in an entire recording, in which case the sound should be concisely described and placed within a set of two open and close parentheses (i.e., the convention for analyst notes). With CA, GAT, and SBS, the convention for analyst notes is also used to describe any noteworthy phenomena. For example, in Extract 49, line 3, an inaudible sound is transcribed by identifying the feature in question.

(49) 1   (7.2)
     2 Peter: there it is, it's this way
     3   ((inaudible))

4.4.7 Unintelligible speech

Transcribing communication data is challenging for many reasons. Sometimes talk is recorded in public spaces, so various background noises result in unintelligible speech. In other recording situations, poorly placed equipment leads to faint voices. Furthermore, accents can be difficult to comprehend, and the speed of communication too challenging to follow. These difficulties and challenges are often exacerbated in multi-party interaction, where overlapping utterances can lead to further hearing troubles. Fortunately, conventions exist to account for difficult-to-hear utterances.

In addition to using analyst notes to highlight difficult-to-hear utterances, researchers have two conventions for representing unintelligible speech: unintelligible syllable and hearing approximations.

4.4.7.1 *Unintelligible syllable*
Completely incomprehensible words and utterances are transcribed by marking each syllable. Transcribing each syllable that makes up the unintelligible speech maintains some representation of the flow of communication. This is particularly helpful during overlapping utterances, where each transcribed syllable provides important information regarding how the interactants manage their talk and interaction. CA, GAT, and SBS, all use a different notation symbol for marking the syllables that make up unintelligible speech. With CA, the notation symbol used is the 'asterisk' sign, as illustrated in Extract 50, line 51.

Chapter 4. Transcribing interactional and paralinguistic features 69

(50) 49 Merchant   yeh smal, i'll choos a large one
     50   (4.0)
     51 Peter: uhm (.) (anydeng for * * *) (3.0)
     52   he's got a large tee shirt
     53   (12.0)

The three asterisks represents three incomprehensible syllable beats. With GAT, the notation symbol used is a lower case 'x', and with SBS, the notation symbol used is the pound/number sign '#'.

4.4.7.2 *Hearing approximations*

With CA and GAT, utterances that are heard with some uncertainty are transcribed with single open and close parentheses. In Extract 51, line 65, Peter quietly produces what seems to be 'okay'.

(51) 62 Peter: [throw
     63   everything all over place
     64   (1.5)
     65 Peter: °(okay)° can- can↓ we↑ get one
     66   [so it's not like] that?

With SBS, the pound/number sign is placed to the left of the word.

(52) 62 Peter: [throw
     63   everything all over place
     64   (1.5)
     65 Peter: °#okay° can- can↓ we↑ get one
     66   [so it's not like] that?
     67 Merchant: [oh >okay. okay.>]

CHAPTER 5

Transcribing nonverbal conduct

5.1 Introduction

The conventions used for transcribing interactional and paralinguistic features allow researchers to closely capture the varied ways in which spoken communication is organized. The conventions discussed in the previous chapter cover a broad spectrum of paralinguistic features that are used to construct meaning and perform social action. Transcribing interactional and paralinguistic features is a prerequisite for developing an understanding of spoken communication in its true form, as it is situated in real life activities (Couper-Kuhlen & Selting, 1996). While these conventions represent most of what a researcher needs to transcribe – and as a result investigate – telephone and other forms of disembodied talk, transcribing nonverbal conduct requires a different set of representational tools. In face-to-face and other types of multimodal interaction, nonverbal conduct (e.g., gaze, body posture, pointing, and nodding) is equally as important, prevalent, and multifunctional, as stress, intonation, and voice amplitude (e.g., Streeck, 2008; Singer, Radinsky, & Goldman, 2008; Mondada, 2009). Although speech and nonverbal conduct often occur in unison (see Goodwin, 2000), this chapter deals primarily with the task of transcribing the latter aspect of communication.

When discussing the task of transcribing video recordings, it is useful to make the distinction between nonverbal conduct and behavior. In this book, nonverbal conduct refers specifically to the movements and positions of the body. The extension of an arm and turning of a head are two examples of movements; body posture and physical proximity of interactants are two examples of positions. The task of transcribing video recordings entails making a series of decisions related to the representation of nonverbal conduct. For example, what is the best way to represent an arm extension or turning of a head in a transcript that is largely text-based? While transcribing video recordings involves making representational decisions (e.g., what is the best way to represent the trajectory of an arm extension?), the primary purpose of transcribing video recordings is to investigate the social and/or interactional significance of nonverbal conduct (e.g., what social action does the arm extension perform?). It could be said that researchers transcribe nonverbal conduct, but their analytic observations are fundamentally concerned with understanding nonverbal behavior. With this in mind, nonverbal behavior refers specifically to the social and interactional meaning that is generated as a result of conduct. Accordingly, transcribing video recordings not only requires knowing how to represent nonverbal conduct in text and/or visual form, but also understanding why a particular movement or position must be transcribed. Typically, the decision to transcribe nonverbal conduct is based on an interest in analyzing a specific nonverbal behavior. That is to say, researchers often use their analytic aims and interests (of nonverbal behavior) to selectively transcribe nonverbal conduct (cf. professional vision; see Goodwin, 1994). For example, investigating turn-taking practices (i.e., behavior) may result in selectively transcribing gaze and head movements (i.e., conduct). It can be said that a researcher must have an understanding of nonverbal behavior before transcribing nonverbal conduct. Indeed, valuable transcription time can be saved when a researcher knows precisely what nonverbal conduct is relevant to a particular analytic aim.

While an understanding of nonverbal behavior is an important part of transcribing video recordings – in that this understanding provides the basis for choosing what nonverbal conduct will be transcribed – the primary objective of this chapter is to review the methods used to transcribe body movements and positions. The decision to focus on the methods used to transcribe nonverbal conduct is based on the belief that the discussion of nonverbal behavior is, by and large, an analytic issue. Indeed, many studies and book-length publications that analyze nonverbal behavior are widely available (e.g., Goodwin, 1981; Kendon, 2004; Streeck, 2008), and should be referred to for more comprehensive and extended discussions and references pertaining to the empirical utility of examining nonverbal aspects of communication. Postgraduate students and researchers with little to no knowledge of nonverbal behavior are encouraged to review the literature before transcribing video recordings. However, when appropriate, references to, and discussions of, these studies will be provided below.

The methods discussed in this chapter do not require using specialized transcription software, though some basic programs are needed (i.e., word processor, media player, graphics editor). Many advantages exist in using basic software programs to transcribe nonverbal conduct. For instance, the basic programs that are needed to transcribe nonverbal conduct are often preloaded onto computers, and require relatively little specialized software knowledge to use. More importantly, basic software programs create transcripts and visual media in highly portable file extensions, allowing researchers to share transcription documents and media across many platforms and academic audiences. Despite these advantages, specialized transcription programs offer numerous sophisticated representational (and analytic tools) that cannot be found in basic software programs, though these tools generally require extensive training to use. Comprehensive user manuals for specialized transcription software are freely available online, and provide program specific information and instruction for researchers in need of more complex tools (for a brief discussion of transcription software, see Section 6.3.6).

This chapter is organized in three sections: nonverbal conduct, media used to represent nonverbal conduct, and methods used to represent sequentiality (i.e., capturing movements as they unfold during communication). The first section identifies six nonverbal (conduct) categories that are commonly seen in transcripts of video recordings. The second section identifies four media used to represent nonverbal conduct, and discusses the benefits and weaknesses of each medium. Finally, the third section identifies four methods used to represent the sequentiality and trajectory of nonverbal conduct.

5.2 Nonverbal conduct

Most communication is intertwined with nonverbal conduct. While this fact is widely known, most studies of talk and interaction are concerned with the spoken aspects of communication. This preoccupation with spoken communication continues despite research indicating that nonverbal conduct is crucial to shaping social activities and co-constructing meaning. For example, Goodwin (2000; 2003) shows how archaeologists accomplish excavation tasks through a complex semiotic interplay between talk and gesture. Through his analysis of excavation dig sites, Goodwin (2003) shows how spoken communication comprises not only words and utterances, but is also intricately coordinated with nonverbal conduct. With the delivery of words and utterances, nonverbal conduct helps interactants organize and make sense of their communicative environments. For example, a hand gesture used at an excavation site helps interactants simultaneously manage a complex task-based conversation and the precise physical dig locations that the talk is referring to. In other words, nonverbal conduct is shaped by, and shapes, those material and semiotic objects – a book, professional practice, cultural tradition, or pen, to name a few – that are immediately relevant for the interactants. The social-interactional importance of nonverbal conduct is not limited to archaeologists. A quick scan of the literature reveals a wide and diverse range of communicative contexts that shape, and are shaped by, nonverbal conduct. For instance, Lazaraton (2004) shows how hand gestures are central to vocabulary explanations in language classrooms, while Keating and Sunakawa (2010) reveal how 'gamers' use body positions and movements to simultaneously negotiate their physical surroundings and virtual online world.

Accordingly, talk and interaction should not be understood from a single mode of communication (Goodwin, 2003). Transcribing video recordings requires being aware of the fact that nonverbal conduct is an omnipresent aspect of communication. Furthermore, body movements and positions possess varying degrees of importance, and the social functions they perform vary from one communicative context to another. For example, the use of gaze may be less important to managing speakership in dyadic conversations than in multi-party discussions. Thus, the challenge in transcribing video recordings stems from the need to first establish an understanding of what movements and positions are especially important for the communicative setting and issues under investigation, and then using this understanding to capture/transcribe nonverbal conduct in a way that allows for fruitful analytic observations. Again, this chapter deals primarily with the latter issue.

Before discussing the methods used to transcribe video recordings (see Sections 5.3 and 5.4), this section will identify six categories of nonverbal conduct that are commonly transcribed: body postures, facial expressions, gestures, gaze, proximity, and actions. It is important to note that these categories do not represent an exhaustive list of conduct that can be transcribed (cf. Kendon, 2004). The purpose of identifying these categories is to show that in any given stretch of communication, there are many types of body movements and positions. That is to say, nonverbal conduct is both complex and diverse. Nonverbal conduct is complex in that there are innumerable ways in which it is used with spoken communication, and diverse in that there are countless variations in which it is 'deployed'. To demonstrate this, a single video still will be used to discuss nonverbal conduct. When appropriate, some discussions of, and references to, studies that examine the social-interactional significance of nonverbal conduct will be provided in order to further highlight the important link between transcription and analysis. Illustration 5.1 will be used as a point of reference for each of the six categories identified below.

Illustration 5.1 Nonverbal communication

5.2.1 Body postures

Body postures are often associated with sitting and standing positions, but can also include leaning, squatting, lying, and kneeling, to name a few. Positions of body do not change during communication as frequently as other forms of nonverbal conduct (e.g., gaze and gestures). However, this does not mean that body postures are not as dynamic and significant to co-constructing meaning.

In Illustration 5.1, for example, Peter is leaning slightly forward, a body position that may be a way of showing that he is actively engaged in the conversation. Also note the merchant's bending posture, a position that is in contrast with Peter's upright posture. While both interactants are in different body positions, they are attending to each other's spoken words. The merchant does this by turning her head over to Peter, while Peter's torso is slightly tilted to his right. This illustration provides a vivid example of how interactants use their bodies to coordinate their talk and physical surroundings. Peter browses the store and the merchant searches for merchandise, while both interactants jointly manage the talk of buying and selling merchandise.

5.2.2 Facial expressions

Frowns, smiles, grins, and grimaces, are just a few examples of facial expressions. Facial expressions are often transcribed, and discussed analytically in research of nonverbal behavior, as frowns, smiles, and the like, are closely coordinated with spoken communication. A smile may follow a compliment or a report of bad news may lead to a frown. In Illustration 5.1, for example, the merchant responds to Peter's spoken words with a smile. From a transcription point of view, therein lies the methodological challenge. Many instances of facial expressions are explicitly situated in spates of talk, and thus have a sequential organization that is clearly identifiable. The methodological challenge concerns the difficulty in using a combination of text and visual media to capture this sequential organization (i.e., the coordination of talk and facial expressions). As discussed in the methods section of this chapter, representing sequentiality with text and visual media is difficult – and somewhat problematic – because transcription tools can only partially capture the dynamic nature of nonverbal conduct.

5.2.3 Gestures

Gestures are movements of the outer body (e.g., shoulders, eyebrows, eyes, and hands) that convey meaning and/or perform social action. Although gestures can include any part of the outer body, they are often associated with hand and head movements. Examples of hand gestures include, but are not limited to, waves, finger wagging, and pointing. Looking down, up, over the shoulder, and nodding, are only a few examples of head movements. Movements of the hand and head are often transcribed because they – like facial expressions – are explicitly coordinated with talk. Mondada (2007), for example, shows how an ostensibly simple hand gesture – in this case, pointing – is intricately coordinated with talk and turn-taking practices, helps manage the task of providing driving instructions, and is synchronized with the nonverbal (and verbal) conduct of the co-interactant. Similarly, in Illustration 5.1, the merchant has her head turned to Peter, a position that shows she is actively listening to what is being said. Peter also has his head turned in, towards the merchant, a position that allows him to set up the necessary physical alignment to establish eye contact. These gestures occur as a series of unfolding movements, and allow both interactants to attend to each other's talk while carrying out their institutional roles – again, Peter browses the store while the merchant searches for merchandise. Because gestures are articulated and coordinated with other material and semiotic objects at the site of communication, transcribing hand and head movements requires knowing what role they play in the larger social setting. As Mondada (2007, p. 815) aptly puts it, "transcripts are produced along with the analysis, and not previously to it."

5.2.4 Gaze

Gaze is the direction in which an interactant is looking. The focal point of a gaze is often on a speaker or recipient, though gaze direction varies – sometimes considerably – according to setting and communicative context. Mutual gaze – a situation where both speaker(s) and listener(s) establish eye contact – often appears in transcripts of communication data because of its close association with turn-taking practices (cf. Goodwin, 2001). As with all other forms of nonverbal conduct, the trajectory and direction of gaze is closely coordinated with other movements, positions, and objects. For example, in Illustration 5.1, the merchant has her head turned towards Peter – despite bending over to look for merchandise – in order to establish eye contact with Peter. Peter – the current speaker in Illustration 5.1 – has his head turned to the merchant, but has not yet established eye contact with her. In addition to body movements and positions, gaze is an important organizing feature of social actions and activities. Sidnell (2009), for instance, shows how gaze is used to carry out and make sense of the telling and listening of stories in conversations. Specifically, gaze direction helped interactants initiate, and attend to, activity shifts between the narrations and reenactments that occur in storytelling.

5.2.5 Proximity

The spatial distance between interactants is another type of nonverbal conduct that may provide important information to an analysis of talk and interaction. The proximity of interactants can provide contextually important information pertaining to the intimacy of the interactants, the topic of discussion, and the formality of the setting, to name a few. In other situations, as in Illustration 5.1, the physical size of the setting may force interactants into specific spatial locations. Note the distance between Peter and the merchant in relation to their surroundings. The relatively small store creates little space between Peter and the merchant. This confined space may, in turn, influence the way Peter and the merchant interact, both verbally and nonverbally.

5.2.6 Actions

Actions are a series of unfolding nonverbal movements and/or positions that are often coordinated with material and semiotic objects (e.g., shaking hands, exchanging merchandise, opening a door, and turning on a computer). Although actions are typically coordinated with talk, they do not always unfold during the act of spoken communication. Opening a door, for instance, involves a series of nonverbal movements and positions, but this action is not always performed as a result of, and/or during, spoken communication. It is useful to think of actions while transcribing video recordings, as body movements and positions are part of larger episodes of social events (cf. Goodwin, 2000; 2003). For example, a gaze is rarely just a single direction in which an interactant is looking; it is closely coordinated with other material and semiotic objects, possesses a trajectory, and performs the social action of managing turns at talk, among other things.

In Illustration 5.1, the merchant is performing the action of searching for merchandise, a response to Peter's interest in purchasing a shirt. The merchant's action – in this particular instance – consists of, but is not limited to, bending over (i.e., body posture), turning the head (i.e., gesture), gazing at Peter (i.e., gaze), and smiling (i.e., facial expression). Capturing actions with visual media allows researchers to discuss the complex interplay between talk, nonverbal conduct, and the social context in which communication takes places. For example, Illustration 5.1 shows that the merchant is searching for merchandise with her arm while facing Peter and attending to his spoken words. A researcher may wish to explore whether these movements and positions are characteristic of doing merchandise selling in this particular location, or whether similar nonverbal conduct occurs in different communicative settings and contexts.

The six categories introduced in this section provide a glimpse into the types of nonverbal conduct that can be transcribed for the analysis of video recordings. The categories show that a single video still possesses many types of nonverbal conduct. Because nonverbal conduct is complex and varied, researchers must approach the task of transcribing video recordings with an understanding of why a particular movement or position must be transcribed. In other words, a researcher should not randomly transcribe nonverbal conduct with the hopes that the transcript will shed light on some empirical issue.

Because it is beyond the scope of this section – and indeed this book – to make connections between research traditions and nonverbal conduct, readers are encouraged to explore the growing body of literature that examines the social-interactional characteristics of nonverbal communication: Goodwin's (1981) seminal book-length study of nonverbal turn-taking behavior is an excellent starting point. Again, knowing what nonverbal conduct should be included in a transcript requires understanding the empirical value of transcribing a particular body movement or position. Once armed with this information, researchers can then identify what transcription method(s) will be used, the topic of discussion for the remaining chapter.

Specifically, the remaining chapter discusses how to transcribe the categories of nonverbal conduct identified above. Transcribing nonverbal conduct requires taking into consideration two representational issues: media used to represent nonverbal conduct and methods used to represent sequentiality (i.e., the unfolding of nonverbal conduct). The former issue will be discussed first.

5.3 Media used to represent nonverbal behavior

Representing nonverbal conduct in transcripts presents many challenges. From a historical perspective, the challenge lies in the fact that transcripts were initially created in response to the use of audio recorders. At the time, paper-based transcripts provided a somewhat effective way of capturing the types of data recordings that were being made. Because most recorders at the time did not capture nonverbal conduct, researchers did not have an immediate need to devise comprehensive and detailed transcription conventions for body movements and positions. Despite the fact that digital video recorders are much more widely available than before, the transcription systems used in present day research reflect the audio recorder and its historical role in the human and social sciences.

A second challenge in transcribing nonverbal conduct is the difficulty in representing dynamic movements and positions on paper. Because nearly all research is published in electronic and paper-based journals, nonverbal conduct is – with the exception of a few journals that store video media – represented statically (see, however, Section 5.4, for a discussion of how nonverbal movements are represented in paper-based transcripts). The challenge in present day research – with technological advancements in video recorders and other data capturing devices – is to devise and refine ways of representing nonverbal conduct in paper-based transcripts.

Understanding what media are available is an important first step in transcribing nonverbal conduct. This section identifies and explicates four media used to represent nonverbal conduct in paper-based transcripts: text, video stills, drawings, and digital renderings.

5.3.1 Text

Text is one of the most commonly used media to transcribe nonverbal conduct in paper-based transcripts. Using text to represent nonverbal conduct entails short written descriptions. In many transcription systems (see Appendix C), written descriptions of nonverbal conduct are placed inside a pair of double parentheses. In Extract 1, for example, the nonverbal conduct of the merchant has been transcribed using the convention for 'analyst notes'.

```
(1)    5  Merchant:   hello sir. (0.5)
       6              do↓ you↑ wa↓nna↑ something?
                      ((merchant extends left arm out))
       7              (0.4)
       8  Peter:      walk in here and have a look.
       9  Merchant:   ((inaudible))
                      ((merchant follows Peter into the store))
      10  Peter:      uh:: maybe. <we::ll see< >we'll
                      ((merchant walks in front of, and faces, Peter))
      11  Peter:      see> what we can do
      12  Merchant:   o::kay. (.) no problem
                      ((merchant smiles and looks away))
      13              (0.7)
```

Note that the written descriptions of nonverbal conduct have been placed below the talk – some researchers include written descriptions on the same line, though this approach produces slightly less readable transcripts. To further enhance readability, a different font should be used for written descriptions of nonverbal conduct. In Extract 1, italic font is used to differentiate between verbal and nonverbal communication.

The benefit in using text to transcribe nonverbal conduct is that written descriptions are relatively easy to create, take little time to complete, and save space when compared to other visual capturing methods. However, written descriptions are problematic in that transcribing nonverbal conduct requires long written description, which in turn lead to muddled transcripts. While avoiding long written descriptions may enhance the readability of a transcript, short written descriptions do not adequately capture the complex nature of nonverbal movements and positions. For example, when the merchant extends her arm in line 6, it is not just the arm that is moving. Other nonverbal movements associated with extending the arm include, but are not limited to, gaze, body posture, and proximity.

Furthermore, researchers must be aware of the granularity of their written descriptions. Does the merchant simply 'extend her arm', or is she 'beckoning to Peter' (see Extract 2). Both descriptions are stylistically different. However, style is not the only issue related to the granularity of written descriptions. The latter description is more interpretive, in that it tells the readers that the merchant is encouraging Peter to enter her store space, while the former description is slightly more open to interpretation in that the arm extension could simply be her way of asking Peter a question.

```
(2)  5   Merchant:    hello sir. (0.5)
     6                do↓ you↑ wa↓nna↑ something? ((merchant extends
                      left arm out, and looks at Peter, while slightly
                      leaning back))
     7                (0.4)
```

Because several representational problems are associated with using written descriptions, visual media methods should be used whenever possible (see, however, Section 5.4.1, for a discussion of how lines can be used to effectively represent the unfolding of gaze).

5.3.2 Video stills

Video stills – also known as still images – are pictures taken from video recordings. For reasons identified below, video stills are a good alternative to written descriptions when nonverbal conduct is the focal point of analysis. Many commercially available software programs have the capability of producing video stills. Furthermore, many free, open-source video players that provide similar picture-capturing capabilities are available online (for a discussion of the ways in which transcription software is used to transcribe and analyze video recordings, see Section 6.3.6). Illustration 5.2 is an example of a video still taken from the same communicative exchange presented in Extracts 1 and 2 above.

When compared to written descriptions, video stills provide rich illustrations of nonverbal conduct. However, the video still on its own does not provide any information regarding what is being said. One way of incorporating the spoken

Illustration 5.2 Video still example

component of this encounter is to enter the text directly onto the video still with a graphics editor program. This method provides an effective way of capturing the talk that is coordinated with the nonverbal conduct. It is not advisable to add text for longer stretches of communication, as this would require covering most of the video still with text and/or reducing the font to a size that is difficult to read. A further disadvantage of typing directly onto video stills is related to the ability to make changes to the embedded text. Most basic graphics editor programs do not provide an easy way of making changes to the text once the video still is saved, and can indeed require creating a new video still.

An equally effective method for adding text to images of nonverbal conduct is to place the talk below or above the video still. For example, in Extract 3, the text is placed above the video still.

```
(3)  5   Merchant:    hello sir. (0.5)
     6                do↓ you↑ wa↓nna↑ something?
```

The visual presentation of nonverbal conduct allows readers to come to their own conclusions regarding how body movements and positions are situated in the context of communication, rather than rely on what is selectively described in writing (cf. the issue of granularity in text descriptions). A key disadvantage in using video stills, however, is that they consume a considerable amount of storage (and page) space, which can in turn make transporting and sharing transcripts difficult. Despite video stills providing a visual medium from which detailed analyses of nonverbal conduct can be made, video stills provide snap shots of body movements and positions. In the words, video stills do not fully capture nonverbal conduct as it is situated and unfolds in communication. A further representational problem surfaces when incorporating video stills with transcripts of spoken communication (cf. Extract 3). While spoken communication is presented as a sequential phenomenon (as represented in line numbers), body movements and positions are represented statically. Consequently, video stills are temporally unaligned with the line-by-line representation of talk (for a discussion of how to transcribe the sequentiality of nonverbal conduct, see Section 5.4). Most transcription programs, however, have the capability of temporally aligning nonverbal conduct with talk (for a discussion of transcription software features, see Section 6.3.6). Accordingly, it is not uncommon to see researchers use screenshots of transcription programs during conference presentations and for research dissemination.

5.3.3 Drawings

Another approach to visually representing nonverbal conduct is to draw the interactants and the physical communicative setting. Drawings of nonverbal conduct are produced if the researcher has not been given ethical clearance to publish video stills and/or if the identities of people and places must be anonymized. Drawings are also used if the researcher has no access to video editing software and/or specialist training in digital editing. Although Illustration 5.3 has been produced with a graphics editor program, drawings can be made freehand and later digitally scanned or alternatively sketched with a basic paint/drawing program.

Drawings of nonverbal conduct offer the same benefits (and pose similar problems) as video stills. However, drawings vary greatly in detail and quality. If drawings must be used, then it is crucial to fully capture those features of nonverbal conduct that are analytically important (see, for example, the hand gesture of the merchant in Illustration 5.3). In more complex settings – which may include multi-party interaction or communication in public spaces – drawings are difficult to produce, and are therefore likely to ineffectively capture the appropriate level of nonverbal detail. Despite this limitation, drawings are relatively easy to produce, and maintain a high level of anonymity for the interactants under investigation.

Chapter 5. Transcribing nonverbal conduct 83

Illustration 5.3 Drawing example

5.3.4 Digital renderings

It is not uncommon for data recordings to contain sensitive and/or private issues. The interactants that have been recorded may be vulnerable, or the topics of discussion may deal with confidential information. In other situations, institutions impose strict ethical guidelines regarding how data is collected and subsequently analyzed and disseminated. Because many researchers are faced with some or all of these issues, it is common practice to conceal the identity of the interactants when transcribing (see also Section 5.3.3). One way of doing this is to digitally render video stills so that it is impossible to identify the interactants under investigation. For instance, in Illustration 5.4, the video still has been embossed in order to obscure the faces of the interactants.

As with drawings, researchers must sacrifice some detail of nonverbal conduct when digitally rendering video stills. For example, compare the detail of the merchant's hand gesture in Illustrations 5.2 – 5.4.

Most graphics editing programs allow researchers to manipulate a video still in a number of different ways. For example, in Illustration 5.5, the video still has been rendered with a series of whirls.

While personal preference generally determines what digital manipulation process will be used, it should be noted that each digitally rendered video still differs in terms of the level of anonymity provided. For example, the colors in

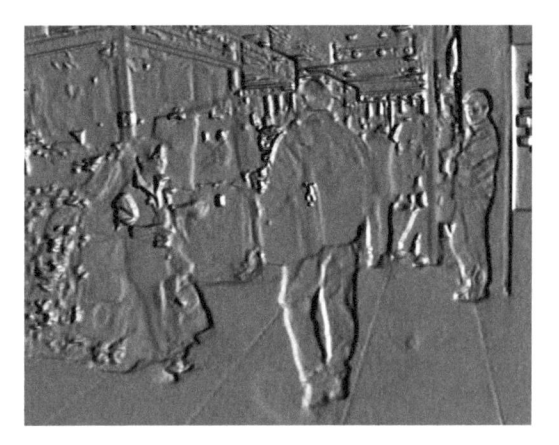

Illustration 5.4 Embossed video still example

Illustration 5.5 Whirled video still example

Illustration 5.5 may reveal who the interactants are, and where the interaction is taking place, whereas the embossing in Illustration 5.4 more effectively masks the identity of the interactants. Video stills can also be manipulated in selected areas (e.g., the face or body of an interactant), which is helpful for maintaining a high level of detail while providing anonymity.

5.4 Methods for representing sequentiality

Knowing what media are available for representing nonverbal conduct is an important step in the process of transcribing video recordings. However, as alluded to in the previous section, video stills and other visual media are snap shots of nonverbal conduct that do not represent movements and positions as they unfold during communication. In order to capture movements and positions as they unfold during communication, researchers must consider a different set of representational issues. Transcribing the sequentiality of nonverbal conduct requires addressing at least one of two representational issues: manner and temporality. Manner as a representational issue concerns how nonverbal conduct is 'done' (i.e., the trajectory of nonverbal conduct). The manner of nonverbal conduct includes the positions and movements of, for example, a hand wave or a head nod. Temporality as a representational issue is related to how nonverbal movements and positions unfold as words are spoken. For example, what is being said as an interactant waves her hand or nods her head?

Four methods for representing sequentiality are discussed in this section: symbols, sequencing, time stamps, and specialist software. Each method covers at least one of the two representational issues (manner and temporality) that researchers must address while transcribing nonverbal conduct.

5.4.1 Symbols

Semi-colons, commas, asterisks, and other symbols can be used to transcribe the sequentiality of nonverbal conduct. This method is commonly used, as it provides a fast and effective way of representing nonverbal conduct. Symbols are also highly flexible in that they can be used in both text-only transcripts and visual media.

In text-only transcripts, symbols show when the nonverbal conduct occurs in relation to the talk. This is accomplished with two symbols. One symbol is used to represent the beginning and end points of nonverbal conduct, and a second symbol corresponds to the nonverbal conduct. For example, in Extract 4, the merchant extends her arm out as she asks a question. The caret symbol '^' is used to represent the beginning and end points of the gestural movement, and the addition symbol '+' corresponds to the gesture. The symbols are placed on a separate line (7a) in order to make it easier to visualize how the gesture unfolds as the question is being asked.

```
(4)   5   Merchant:   hello sir.
      6               (0.5)
      7               do↓ you↑ wa↓nna↑ something?
      7a              ^++++++++++++++++++++++++^
      8               (0.4)
      9   Peter:      walk in here and have a look.
```

86   Transcribing talk and interaction

Illustration 5.6 Gaze

Although the caret and addition symbols used in Extract 4 show when the gesture occurs in relation to the talk – thus addressing the representational issue of temporality – the symbols do not illustrate the manner of nonverbal conduct.

In order to show the manner of nonverbal conduct, researchers must use symbols in visual media. For example, in Illustration 5.6, two arrows are embedded in a video still in order to represent the gaze of the two interactants.

In Illustration 5.6, a large arrow is used to represent the merchant's gaze, while a smaller arrow corresponds to Peter's gaze. Both arrows illustrate the manner of gaze, but do not show how the gaze unfolds as words are spoken. In order to accurately transcribe the manner of nonverbal conduct as talk unfolds (i.e., address both the issue of manner and temporality), two or more video stills must be used with a text transcript (see Section 5.4.3).

5.4.2 Sequencing

A second way of representing the manner of nonverbal conduct is to sequence video stills. Sequencing requires merging two or more video stills into a single picture. The method of sequencing video stills is particularly useful in capturing the unfolding of several nonverbal movements and/or positions. For instance, in Illustration 5.7, four video stills have been merged into a single picture. The sequence effectively shows how Peter's gaze, body position, and head movement, change or unfold over the course of four video stills.

When sequencing, researchers should number each video still in order to help readers follow the events unfold. Numbering video stills offers a fast and relatively effective way of representing positions and movements, though researchers who require a more precise method of representing the manner of nonverbal conduct should use time stamps in lieu of numbers (see Section 5.4.3). As with other visual

Illustration 5.7 Sequencing example

media, adding text above or below the sequencing example allows researchers to capture the temporality of nonverbal conduct.

5.4.3 Time stamps

The method of time stamps entails marking body positions and movements with 'measured' readings of when nonverbal conduct occurs. Time stamps are measured readings in that software programs are used to determine the precise point in which a movement or position occurs in a recording. Time stamps can be used for both text-only transcripts and visual media.

For text-only transcripts, time stamps should be used with a set of notation symbols, as discussed in Section 5.4.1. In Extract 5, for example, time stamps have been added to the moment when the merchant extends her arm as she asks a question (see Extract 4). Again, the caret symbol represents beginning and end points, and the addition symbol represents the gesture.

```
(5)    5   |19.3~20.0|   Merchant:   hello sir.
       6                              (0.5)
       7   |20.5~21.3|                do↓ you↑ wa↓nna↑ something?
       7a                             ^20.6++++++++++++++21.2^
       8                              (0.4)
       9   |21.7-22.7|   Peter:       walk in here and have a
      10                              look.
```

In line 7a, the time stamps show that the merchant begins to extend her arm at the 20.6-second mark of the recording, and ends at the 21.2-second mark. The time stamps show that the merchant initiates her question before she begins to extend her arm, and terminates the arm extension gesture before she ends her question.

In Extract 6, time stamps have also been added to each utterance in order to represent the temporality of the gesture in relation to the talk. For example, in line 5, the exchange begins at the 19.3-second mark of the recording, when the merchant initiates a greeting, and the exchange ends in line 10, at the 22.7-second mark, when Peter ends his respond to the merchant's question. Note that while the time stamps here provide a more accurate representation of temporality than the symbol-only method used in Extract 4, time stamps do not address the representational issue of manner of nonverbal conduct.

In order to transcribe the manner of nonverbal conduct using time stamps, researchers must use a sequence of video stills, as in Extract 6.

```
(6)  5   |19.3~20.0|   Merchant:   hello sir.
     6                              (0.5)
     7   |20.5~21.3|                do↓ you↑ wa↓nna↑ something?
```

In this example, a text transcript has been included to show how the gesture is situated in the spoken exchange. The first video still has been taken from the 20.0-second mark of the recording, and corresponds to the end of the merchant's greeting in line 5. The second video still has been taken from the 21.1-second mark of the recording, and corresponds to the moment before the merchant ends her question in line 7. The sequence of video stills illustrates what the merchant is doing nonverbally, before she extends her arm, and what she is doing nonverbally moments before she ends her question.

In terms of detail and accuracy, time stamped video stills used in conjunction with text-based transcripts provide the best method for representing the dynamic nature of nonverbal conduct. Although this method is time-consuming (for discussion of how transcription software can save time in representing nonverbal conduct, see Section 6.3.6), the benefits gained from being able to precisely analyze body positions and movements far outweigh the costs of spending long hours transcribing the manner and temporality of nonverbal conduct.

CHAPTER 6

Advanced issues

6.1 Introduction

Many theoretical and practical transcription issues have been addressed in this book. While the issues identified in previous chapters cover most of what is needed to carry out the task of transcribing talk and interaction, some research aims and/or data recordings require addressing and/or taking into consideration issues that have hitherto not been discussed. The aim of this chapter is to identify and explicate these transcription issues. The issues identified in this chapter are advanced in that the discussions go beyond the foundational topics reviewed in previous chapters, while at the same time addressing more specialized topics. Though it is impossible to identify all potentially relevant transcription issues that have not been reviewed thus far, the topics discussed in this chapter sufficiently cover a broad range of issues and transcription scenarios.

In the interest of organizational simplicity, the chapter is divided into two sections: theoretical and practical issues. The advanced theoretical section addresses issues that provide a better overall understanding of transcribing communication data, whereas the advanced practical section identifies issues that are specific to the task of transcribing.

6.2 Advanced theoretical issues

The task of transcribing communication data is fundamentally about making decisions regarding how to represent talk and interaction. How much detail should be added to a transcript? What approach will be used to transcribe accents, dialects, and language varieties? What ethical guidelines must be followed in presenting personal names? The issues raised in these questions affect how transcripts are read and analyzed. While Chapter 2 discussed how representational issues are underpinned by a researcher's empirical interests, disciplinary background, and theoretical assumptions, little has been said about how a researcher's level of involvement in transcribing communication data influences what ultimately appears in a transcript. Involvement levels are important to a better overall understanding of transcribing, as researchers vary in how much time and energy they put into the 'final' product, but few are explicitly aware of what impact their involvement

<--- High involvement ———— Low involvement --->

Figure 6.1 Involvement continuum

has on what appears in a transcript. Involvement levels vis-à-vis transcribing communication data are best represented along a continuum, as illustrated in Figure 6.1.

High involvement refers to the situation where researchers completely immerse themselves in all aspects of transcription work. The researcher is the transcriber, and vice versa. The researcher/transcriber spends long hours and many months (or even years) transcribing communication data, and is responsible for all decisions pertaining to representational issues. Low involvement, on the other hand, refers to the situation where the researcher focuses on other aspects of the research process (e.g., gathering other forms of data and doing a literature review of the study), while a specialist carries out the transcription work. In other words, the researcher and transcriber are different people. The researcher spends few hours – if any at all – transcribing communication data, and the transcriber – not the researcher – is responsible for most aspects of transcription work.

This section will discuss three issues that are important to an understanding of how involvement levels shape what and how communication data is transcribed: myopia, present and recall, and outsourcing. Each of the three issues discussed correspond to a different level of involvement. Myopia corresponds to high involvement levels, somewhere in the middle of the continuum lies present and recall, and the issue of outsourcing relates to low involvement levels. Each issue will be discussed in this order.

6.2.1 Myopia

High involvement in transcribing talk and interaction is often encouraged, as being immersed in all aspects of the transcription process promotes greater awareness of the data, leading to better analytic observations. Furthermore, the decision to be involved in most – if not all – aspects of transcription work allows researchers to discuss their transcripts more thoroughly when disseminating research findings. For example, discussing why a word or utterance has been transcribed in a particular way or to what extent a transcript is representative of an entire data set – two questions that are often heard during conference presentations or data workshops – is much easier to do when researchers take the responsibility to oversee the transcription process.

Despite these benefits, there are two problematic situations that may arise as a result of being highly involved in the transcription process: tunnel vision and emotional attachment. Both situations relate to when researchers condition themselves to hear and/or see communication data in a biased way.

6.2.1.1 *Tunnel vision*

Tunnel vision occurs when researchers make representational decisions without carefully considering other transcription options. Tunnel vision can affect anything from the way an utterance is transcribed to how a transcript is organized. Take, for example, the following situation. A researcher is confronted with a word that has two possible hearings: 'excited' and 'excellent'. The researcher decides that 'excited' is the word that should be transcribed. Tunnel vision is the inability to take into consideration the possibility that the decision to transcribe 'excited' was wrong. Researchers who are highly involved in the transcription process are likely to acquire tunnel vision because they spend countless hours making many representational decisions, often in isolation. The image of a researcher hunched over a computer somewhere in a dark basement of a building is all too familiar in the research community. Because these researchers spend long hours, and are solely responsible for, transcribing data recordings, they can easily condition themselves to believe that their decisions are not open to scrutiny. This situation is highly problematic, as any given recording of communication data can be transcribed in a number of different ways.

Researchers can avoid tunnel vision by utilizing resources that provide different perspectives to data recordings and transcripts. Resources that provide different perspectives can be classified into two types: technical and human. An example of a technical resource is media playback software. Researchers can use software to play back data recordings at different speeds (see Chapter 3). This may help, for example, in hearing an utterance spoken softly in a busy public space, say at a cafe or dinner table, or when transcribing poorly recorded data.

An example of a human resource is a colleague or transcription specialist. Human resources are effective in avoiding tunnel vision in that a colleague or transcription specialist brings a different set of skills and experience to the task of transcribing data recordings. For instance, a highly experienced transcription specialist will likely have greater acoustic sensitivity, and therefore approach the listening of difficult-to-hear words and utterances differently than a less experienced researcher. A colleague may be equally helpful in deciphering words and utterances if he or she is an expert in the language and/or setting and context under investigation. It is important to have access to human resources because researchers can quickly convince themselves that what they are hearing in a data recording is exactly what is being said (Duranti, 2006).

Because even one incorrectly transcribed word or utterance can change the way a transcript is read, researchers must take advantage of technical and/or human resources. A researcher is more likely to accurately transcribe a difficult-to-hear word or utterance if presented with two or more perspectives. Although it is common practice to use technical resources to transcribe data recordings (e.g., playback software), human resources are not exploited to the same extent. In order to avoid tunnel vision, researchers must not only make use of technical resources, but they should also frequently subject their transcripts to human scrutiny. Human scrutiny can come in the form of a data workshop with a small group of close colleagues or as a conference presentation to a much larger audience. While there are no established transcription guidelines regarding the use of human resources, data-sharing workshops and presentations should be regularly integrated into the transcription process.

6.2.1.2 *Emotional attachment*

High involvement can also result in developing an emotional attachment to data recordings and/or transcripts. Developing an emotional attachment to data recordings and transcripts is problematic for the same reasons identified in the discussion of tunnel vision. In short, emotional attachment can lead to the situation where researchers condition themselves to hear and see data recordings in a biased, unproductive way.

Emotional attachment occurs when researchers immerse themselves in the transcribing process so much that they begin to establish a personal bond with the interactants under investigation. The storied lives of the interactants – their life decisions and thoughts – become a part of the researcher's world. Because of this, it is not uncommon for researchers to, for example, judge the morality of the interactants, take sides if an argument ensues, or provide solutions to life problems. While formulating a personal opinion is a natural, human response to hearing an interesting stretch of talk or watching a series of events unfold, researchers must not let their emotions influence their representational decisions. This requires researchers to be cognizant of the emotional values they place on the interactants and setting under investigation. However, being aware of how emotions shape transcripts is not enough to prevent researchers from hearing and seeing data recordings in a biased, unproductive way. As with tunnel vision, researchers must also subject their transcripts to human scrutiny. This is because colleagues and the larger research community will be less emotionally attached, have different emotional responses to the data recording, and are therefore more likely to provide alternative perspectives to how the data should be transcribed.

Researchers can also develop an emotional attachment to transcripts. Transcripts are products of many hours logged listening to, and watching, data recordings. Therefore, the time and energy spent producing transcripts has an emotional value. This emotional value means that each representational decision made whilst transcribing has a history of some sort. For example, a researcher will not only remember why a word or utterance was transcribed in a particular way, but also the time and resources used to make the representational decision. The emotional values associated with, and histories of, these decisions create a strong sense of ownership. While having a strong sense of ownership is one of the many benefits of being highly involved in the transcription process, this feeling can lead to tunnel vision if a researcher allows the emotion and history of a decision to get in the way of different perspectives (see Section 6.2.1.1).

6.2.2 Present and recall

In the previous section, it was argued that high involvement levels are generally beneficial for doing transcription work, though researchers should occasionally step back and incorporate different perspectives from technical and human resources. In terms of moderate involvement levels, taking into consideration different perspectives means actively seeking ways to incorporate other ideas and solutions. This can be done in two ways: present and recall.

First, researchers can actively seek other ideas and solutions by presenting their data recordings and transcripts to academic audiences at data presentation workshops. In these data sharing workshops – also known as data sessions – researchers find solutions for difficult-to-hear words and utterances, share observations, and resolve different transcription and analytical viewpoints. While there are no rules regarding how a data session should be conducted, a researcher presenting his or her data will benefit the most if all of the session participants contribute to the discussion. Data sessions are meant to enhance an understanding of data recordings, and therefore create better conditions for transcribing talk and interaction. More importantly, data sessions allow researchers to focus on specific stretches of communication that will be later used for research dissemination. Consequently, data sessions perform the important, and necessary, function of fine-tuning a transcript before it is presented to a larger audience.

Second, researchers can actively seek other ideas and solutions by asking the interactants under investigation to recall specific stretches of talk and interaction. As with data sessions, the purpose of recall is not to hand over the responsibility of transcribing to someone else, but rather to develop a better overall understanding of the data recording. The primary aim in using the perspectives of the interactants under investigation is to find solutions for transcribing difficult-to-hear words and utterances. The benefit in using interactants to assist in this endeavor is that they can use their firsthand knowledge of participating in past communicative exchanges to decipher what has been said. While interactants' ability to recall information will vary, they are potentially useful in monitoring high involvement levels and preventing tunnel vision and emotional attachment.

Whether relying exclusively on data sessions with a group of researchers or recall sessions with interactants or a combination of the two, the benefits of taking into consideration different hearings and perspectives far outweigh the advantages of transcribing in isolation. Although research interests and disciplinary traditions will partly determine involvement levels, it is good transcription practice to maximize opportunities to share and present data recordings and transcripts to other peers and colleagues.

6.2.3 Outsourcing

On the other side of the involvement continuum is outsourcing. Outsourcing involves hiring a transcription specialist to take some or all of the responsibility of transcribing. Outsourcing is often done because of time constraints and/or research objectives. Many researchers simply do not have enough time to transcribe, for example, when a funding body sets a tight deadline to complete a research project. In other situations, researchers pass on the responsibility of transcribing because they have the mentality that transcribing is an unnecessary part of doing research (Tilley, 2003). This mentality is driven by the erroneous assumption that transcripts are the primary source of data. However, transcript-based research requires using transcripts in conjunction with data recordings. That is to say, making good transcript-based observations requires having intimate knowledge of data recordings. When researchers outsource their transcription work, they are more likely to treat transcripts as the primary source of data because they are not required to immerse themselves in the recordings. Although outsourcing can lead to detailed transcripts, a true understanding of the interactional nuances and linguistic peculiarities of the interactants under investigation can only be acquired by logging many hours listening to or watching, and then transcribing, data recordings.

While it is advisable to take some responsibility in the transcription process, personal and institutional constraints sometimes dictate how much data – if any at all – will be transcribed. If researchers must outsource their transcription work, then there are two issues that must be taken into consideration: selection of labor and division of labor. Selection of labor is related to who is hired to transcribe data recordings, and division of labor concerns who will transcribe what. When selecting outside help, a researcher has the option of using a company that specializes in transcription work. Outsourcing to a company can be helpful, as most transcription companies can efficiently transcribe large amounts of data in short periods of time. However, transcription companies are unlikely to be aware of – and therefore utilize – the notation symbols discussed in Chapter 5.

Alternatively, a researcher can seek the assistance of someone from inside the research community, say a postgraduate student that is familiar and interested in transcript-based research. Outsourcing transcription work to people within the research community is advantageous in that these people may already know how – and if not, can be trained – to use one or more of the transcription systems discussed previously.

Division of labor is also an important issue in outsourcing transcription work. Outsourcing requires knowing what parts of the transcript will be completed by outside help. A common outsourcing issue concerns identifying who will transcribe the different types/levels of transcription detail. For example, a transcription company can be used to provide an initial, orthographic representation of communication data, and a postgraduate student can be used to provide more detail by using specialized notation symbols for interactional and paralinguistic features. Again, while it is not advisable to outsource all aspects of transcription work, if it is necessary to do so, then labor should be carefully selected and divided according to practical constrains and empirical needs and interests.

6.3 Advanced practical issues

Transcribing is a meticulous task. The foundational topics discussed in Chapter 3, the transcription systems reviewed in Chapter 4, and the multimodal representational issues identified in Chapter 5, all add to the complexities of transcribing communication data. Despite the breath of topics discussed in previous chapters, there are several outstanding practical transcription issues that warrant discussion. This section will identify these issues, and provide examples of how to address them. Some of the discussions in this section provide general suggestions that improve the readability of transcripts (i.e., capitalization and apostrophes), while other discussions are situation-specific in that they are only relevant to certain data recording types (i.e., conversational floors and translations). For example, the issue of conversational floor is more likely to be relevant in recordings of multi-party interaction in that it is not uncommon for one topic of discussion to break into two or more. That is not to say that situation-specific transcription issues are less important than the general suggestions provided in this chapter. Knowing how to address a broad range of transcription issues – even if the issues are not immediately applicable to existing empirical aims – is crucial to producing transcripts that are accurate representations of data recordings, and providing sound, transcript-based analytic observations. The advanced practical issues discussed below are in no particular order.

6.3.1 Capitalization

Capitalization is the practice of capitalizing words in a transcript. When transcribing, there are two, overlapping reasons why a researcher capitalizes a word. First, a researcher capitalizes a word in order to enhance the readability of a transcript. For example, some researchers believe that capitalizing proper names allows readers to easily identify important information in a transcript. Second, a researcher capitalizes a word in order to follow written conventions. The latter reason will be discussed first.

Transcripts consist of texts and punctuation markers, with specific margin sizes, line spacing, and font type and size. In other words, transcripts are written documents. Accordingly, many researchers intentionally (or unintentionally) follow written conventions when transcribing communication data. For example, in Extract 1, each word that begins a new utterance is capitalized.

```
(1)  5   Merchant:   Hello sir. (0.5) Do↓ you↑
     6               wa↓nna↑ something?
     7               (0.4)
     8   Peter:      Walk in here and have a look.
```

While there is nothing inherently wrong with this approach, capitalizing each word that begins a new utterance is not necessary for three reasons. First, transcripts are representations of talk and interaction. Therefore, the words and utterances spoken in each turn do not represent sentences. Second, capitalization is often reserved for representing emphatic talk (see Chapter 4). Third, capitalizing each word that begins a new utterance (and/or line of talk) does not enhance the readability of transcripts. It is for these reasons that it is advisable to use lowercase letters (see Extract 2), and reserve capital letters for proper names and emphatic talk.

```
(2)  5   Merchant:   hello sir. (0.5) do↓ you↑
     6               wa↓nna↑ something?
     7               (0.4)
     8   Peter:      walk in here and have a look.
```

Because proper names (and pronouns) occur in high frequency, some researchers find it easy to only capitalize emphatic talk. For example, in Extract 3, proper names and pronouns are transcribed in lowercase letters.

```
(3)  88  Peter:      [[so what's your price]]
     89  Merchant:   [[i'll give you a good]] price
     90  Peter:      because last time you- you sold
     91              it for twenty (yuan)
```

Note the pronoun in line 89 and proper name in line 91 are not capitalized. This approach is less likely to create confusion regarding when and how written and transcription conventions are used. However, some researchers argue that the readability of transcripts suffers with this approach, as proper names and pronouns are more difficult to locate and refer to during discussions of data recordings. Accordingly, some researchers choose to capitalize every instance of proper names and/or pronouns, as in Extract 4.

```
(4)  88 Peter:      [[so what's your price]]
     89 Merchant:   [[I'll give you a good]] price
     90 Peter:      because last time you- you sold
     91             it for twenty (Yuan)
```

While the decision to capitalize a particular word is often a matter of personal preference, the decision should not be taken lightly, as approaches to capitalization influence the overall readability of transcripts. Furthermore, while the representational differences between Extracts 3 and 4 may appear minimal, a researcher must understand the consequences of selecting a particular approach to capitalization.

6.3.2 Apostrophes

Like capitalization, the use of apostrophes in transcripts is shaped by written conventions. One approach is to use apostrophes when a word is contracted, as in Extract 5.

```
(5)  188 Merchant:  =i think maybe you're- you're
     189            big boss so small money for you
     190            people
```

While the word spoken by the merchant in the data recording sounds like the possessive adjective 'your', the communicative context reveals that the word is a contraction of 'you are'. Therefore, in line 188, the word is transcribed as 'you're'. The benefit in this approach is that the apostrophe provides a visual representation of the grammatical function of the word. In other words, the apostrophe shows that the merchant is not referring to something Peter is in possession of, which in turn makes it easier for readers to follow the meaning of the interaction. Alternatively, a researcher can strictly adhere to the idea that a transcript is a representation of spoken talk and interaction, and therefore transcribe words and utterances only as they sound (i.e., ignore the grammatical function/meaning of words and utterances; see Extract 6).

```
(6)  188 Merchant:  =i think maybe your- your
     189            big boss so small money for you
     190            people
```

Although this approach more closely represents the sound that is made, it ignores the meaning of the word, and the fact that a transcript is a hybrid document that follows both written and spoken conventions.

As with literary writing, apostrophes can also add 'color' to a transcript. For example, in Extract 7, the use of apostrophes in lines 231 and 233 captures the pronunciation of the merchant.

```
(7) 231  Merchant:  no. [just'a-       ]
    232  Peter:         [that's so kind]
    233  Merchant:  you just'a choose something=
    234  Peter:     =no::: no no it's alright=
```

Care should be taken when using apostrophes in this way, as adding 'color' to transcripts may caricaturize the interactants (for further discussion, see Chapter 2). While it is good transcription practice to accurately represent the sounds and interaction of data recordings, researchers must be cognizant of the social and political impact representational decisions have on the interactants.

6.3.3 Conversational floors

A conversational floor consists of two or more speakers participating in one topic of discussion. In some communicative settings – say a large family dinner – there may be two or more simultaneous conversational floors. While the left-to-right and top-to-bottom layout used in most transcripts is conducive for transcribing one conversational floor (see Chapter 3), this layout is less effective when representing two or more conversational floors. For example, in Extract 8, the left-to-right and top-to-bottom layout is used to represent the discussion of three interactants.

```
(8) 14  Chris:     you↓ don't↑ remember him?
    15             (1.2)
    16  Peter:     no:::, we're a[ll
    17  Merchant:                [i remember you
    18  Chris:     o:kay=
    19  Merchant:  =hehehe
    20  Chris:     do you remember he bought=
```

Close examination of this extract reveals that the interaction is primarily between Chris and the merchant. Chris asks a question to the merchant, the merchant answers, Chris then provides an acknowledgement token, the merchant follows with laughter, and finally Chris asks the merchant a second question. While Peter attempts to take part in the exchange, his contribution is not treated as topically relevant. However, the layout of Extract 8 does little in the way of helping the reader appreciate the fact that Chris and the merchant do not respond to Peter's utterance. This is because the talk and interaction is read from left-to-right and top-to-bottom, as if all three interactants are equally involved in the conversational floor. Now compare Extract 8 with Extract 9.

```
(9)          Main floor                        Sub-floor
     14 Chris:   you↓ don't↑
     15          remember him?
     16          (1.2)
                                        17 Peter:  no:::, we're a[ll
     18 Merch:  [i remember you
     19 Chris:   o:kay=
     20 Merch:  =hehehe
     21 Chris:   do you remember
     22          he bought=
```

In the interest of simplicity, Peter's utterance has been classified as a 'sub-floor'. In Extract 9, it is easy to see that Peter's talk is not incorporated into the conversation by his fellow interactants. In using two columns, a researcher can visually demonstrate the fact that Peter's utterance is not treated as topically relevant. Furthermore, in recordings of two or more conversational floors, columns allow readers to analyze topics independent of other, topically irrelevant talk. However, from an organizational point of view, columns may present problems when transcribing long utterances and/or three or more conversational floors (for a discussion of these representational issues, see Section 3.3.1).

6.3.4 Translations

When presenting transcripts comprising a language that is not spoken or understood by the intended audience, it is customary to provide at least one translation. In Extract 10, for example, the language of the recording (English) is presented with two types of (Korean) translations: literal and idiomatic.

```
(10)  71 Merchant:  how    much you  want?
                    얼마나 많이  당신 원하다?
                    얼마 내고 싶어요
      72            (0.5)
      73 Peter:     how    much do   i  want=
                    얼마나 많이  하다 나 원하다=
                    내가 얼마 내고 싶으냐고요
```

The first Korean line is a literal (direct), word-for-word translation. This type of translation allows readers to understand what has been said without any syntactic and semantic modifications. Word-for-word translations are also useful in examining the theoretical and descriptive aspects of language. The second translation provides an idiomatic representation of the recorded language. This type of translation is included to convey the meaning of the recorded talk, as it would be understood naturally in the translated language. If two translations are provided in a transcript, then one translation should be italicized to enhance readability. In Extract 11, literal and idiomatic translations are provided in English.

```
(11)  71  Merchant:  얼마 내고 싶어요
                     how pay want
                     how much you want
      72             (0.5)
      73  Peter:     내가 얼마 내고 싶으냐고요
                     i   how pay want
                     how much do i want
```

Minimally, idiomatic translations must be provided so readers will understand how the language is being used. Although literal translations are useful for theoretical and descriptive linguists, they reveal less pragmatic and social meaning. However, with that said, idiomatic translations must retain the pragmatic and social meaning of the recorded talk, a task that is particularly difficult – in some cases and for some languages, impossible – to achieve.

6.3.5 Add-on conventions

Researchers are occasionally confronted with paralinguistic and/or interactional phenomena that have no record of being transcribed in previous research. This is likely to occur when investigating new and emerging settings (e.g., technology-mediated communication), and/or because empirical aims and interests dictate a unique research focus. In these situations, it is common practice to develop a new notation symbol for the phenomenon under investigation. While there are no established guidelines regarding how to select notation symbols for transcription purposes, researchers should not select a symbol that has been used to represent an existing paralinguistic and/or interactional phenomenon (see Chapter 5, for commonly used notation symbols). It should also be noted that some symbols are not compatible across different software programs and computers. Therefore, compatibility and portability must be taken into consideration when selecting a new symbol (for a discussion of font type, see Section 3.4.1).

6.3.6 Transcription software

With continuous advancements in computer technology, it is now common practice to use software to transcribe data recordings. However, great variation exists in the degree to which software is used to assist in transcription work. The most minimal use of software involves creating transcripts with word processing programs. Although word processing programs are not specifically designed for transcribing communication data, they provide flexible and easy-to-use computer-assisted tools for representing talk and interaction. Margin sizes, line numbers, line spacing, and font type, to name a few, are fully adjustable, and require little training to use (see Chapter 3). Furthermore, transcripts created with word processing programs are highly portable in that documents can be saved easily in a number of different, highly compatible file extensions. Most researchers are familiar with the features of word processing programs, and are content with using them to transcribe data recordings.

Despite the utility of word processing programs, more and more transcripts today are being created with specialized transcription software. Numerous programs are available for transcribing communication data. Some of the most widely used transcription programs can be downloaded at no cost, and provide manuals that comprehensively detail operational features and issues (see below). Because these programs offer complex computer-assisted transcription tools that can only be learned through reading user manuals and hands-on experience, this section will not discuss how to use transcription programs, nor will it review and recommend those programs that are commonly used. Indeed, such a discussion would require an entire book dedicated to the overview of computer-assisted transcription tools. Accordingly, the aim of this section is to identify and discuss features of transcription programs that are helpful in transcribing data recordings, and are not available in most word processing programs. In so doing, it is hoped that readers will be able to make informed decisions regarding whether and which specialized software is needed. When applicable, references to specific transcription programs will be provided. Before proceeding, it is important to reemphasize the fact that transcription programs require extensive hands-on experience, and in some cases, training. This is demonstrated – in part – by the fact that software developers (and experienced users) offer tailored training and workshops at conferences and universities around the world. While transcription programs offer numerous benefits, an initial period of learning is needed before these benefits can be realized.

In most transcription programs, all tasks used for transcribing communication data are contained and managed in one user interface (UI). This ostensibly simple feature has many advantages. The first, and most obvious, benefit relates to how documents and media are managed. Managing all transcription tasks in one UI allows users to play audio/video files while creating transcripts (e.g., ELAN and FOLKER). That is to say, researchers can simultaneously manage two tasks (i.e., playing back data recordings and representing talk and interaction in transcripts) in one graphical window. This feature eliminates the need to run, and toggle between, two programs that serve different purposes. This feature can save time during long transcribing sessions, as transcribing with a word processing program requires using at least one other program to play back data recordings (e.g., Audacity). In addition to saving time from eliminating the need to run, and toggle between, multiple programs, the ability to manage different transcription tasks in one UI simplifies many tasks related to producing and disseminating transcripts. For instance, transcripts produced in most transcription programs are synchronized (temporally aligned) with audio/video media, allowing users to easily find where line numbers in a transcript occur within a data recording. This is especially beneficial when locating, and referring back to, specific points in a transcript, as well as for disseminating research and sharing observations during data workshops and presentations. Conversely, transcribing with word processing programs requires manually entering time stamps on transcripts, and then manually locating its corresponding stretches of communication within data recordings. Manually searching through data can prove difficult and time consuming, especially for longer recordings of communication data. The issue of temporal alignment is particular important when transcribing the sequentiality of nonverbal conduct (see Section 5.4).

Some transcription programs also allow users to categorize data sets (transcripts and audio/video media) according to research interests (e.g., Transana). For example, smaller segments within a single data recording can be categorized into distinct interactional phenomena. This feature effectively allows users to create separate clips within, and across, data recordings. Accordingly, it is not uncommon to see transcription programs being used as a dissemination-and-sharing tool at conferences and workshops. Furthermore, keywords can often be added to, and within, data recordings, a feature that further facilitates the (collaborative) production, analysis, and sharing of transcripts in that users can do keyword searchers through large data sets.

In a similar vein, some programs offer sophisticated computer-assisted tools that allow users to not only create transcripts, but also analyze them. For instance, CLAN (Computerized Language ANalysis) is a program that allows users to create and edit transcripts, as well as conduct frequency counts, search for specific words, and carryout co-occurrence analyses, to name a few (see MacWhinney, 2010a). Transcripts created with CLAN typically use the CHAT transcription system (MacWhinney, 2010b), and are stored in the CHILDES (Child Language Exchange System) database (see also Schmidt & Schütte, 2010, for a discussion of the FOLK corpus and FOLKER transcription program). It should be noted that CLAN transcripts are saved in a unique file extension that cannot be opened with most word processing programs. The issue of saving transcripts in a unique file extension and storing them in a shared database is noteworthy, as most transcription programs produce transcripts in a file extension that is not cross compatible unless converted into a different format (or the contents are copied onto a document that is cross compatible). It is for this reason that many research networks use the same transcription program.

Despite the compatibility problems that may arise as a result of using specialized software, working with the same transcription program (and shared database) promotes quality standardization within research teams/networks. Expectations of what a transcript should look like are more uniform, as members within a team or network utilize the same transcription tools and follow the same software protocols. Uniformity of expectations allows researchers to create large databases where little variation exists from one transcript to another, especially if adopting the same transcription system. This is, of course, beneficial when disseminating and sharing observations and findings to a larger academic audience. Lastly, working with the same transcription program makes it easier to develop guidelines for good transcription practice; thus, researchers can more easily uphold quality standards by sharing the same approach to transcribing communication data.

While this section has not provided a comprehensive overview of software features, the discussion of transcription programs should provide enough information to make an initial decision regarding whether a word processing program or specialized software is needed. Word processing programs provide a quick and easy solution to transcribing data recordings. Word processing programs allow researchers with little to no transcription experience and knowledge to begin transcribing soon after data collection, as little technical knowledge is needed in using these programs. Conversely, even the most primary function of a transcription program requires an initial period of learning. For instance, creating a new document – a task that is easily accomplished in a word processing program – requires understanding how a transcription program uniquely creates, stores, retrieves, and manages transcripts. Researchers working with tight deadlines may see this initial period of learning as problematic, and thus avoid using specialized software. For many researchers, however, the benefits of using software that provides complex transcription and analytic tools far outweigh the steep learning curve involved in mastering a transcription program.

6.4 Conclusion

Interest in transcript-based research has grown significantly in recent years. Alongside this growth has been an increase in awareness of the empirical utility of naturalistic research on language use in interaction. Despite interest in, and awareness of, transcript-based analyses of communication, relatively few discussions have, and are, taking place with regard to how transcripts evolve into the products that are later used to produce and disseminate research. Given the number of book-length publications devoted to conducting transcript-based research, it seems necessary to scrutinize the theories and practices of transcription work. However, researchers must not only scrutinize the 'finished' products that show up in the data analysis sections of research publications. Greater attention must also be placed on the process of producing transcripts. Transcribing is a situated practice (Mondada, 2007), and therefore transcripts are reflexively tied to the innumerable representational and analytic decisions that are made during their production. In other words, transcribing is a process that entails representing talk and interaction, as well as a reflection of empirical aims and interests. Being cognizant of transcription work involves a higher appreciation, awareness, and understanding, of how the text and organization contained within a transcript are shaped by representational and analytic decisions. It is hoped that the discussions and references contained in this book provide the necessary knowledge and skill base to scrutinize these decisions (see Appendix D, for a quick start guide to transcribing).

References

Adolphs, S. (2008). *Corpus and Context: Investigating pragmatic functions in spoken discourse.* Amsterdam: John Benjamins.

Ashmore, M., MacMillan, K., & Brown, S.D. (2004). It's a scream: Professional hearing and tape fetishism. *Journal of Pragmatics*, 36, 349–374.

Atkinson, J.M., & Heritage, J. (Eds.) (1984). *Structures of Social Action: Studies in Conversation Analysis.* Cambridge: Cambridge University Press.

Audacity. Last accessed on 3 January 2011 at: http://audacity.sourceforge.net/

Auer, P. Couper-Kuhlen, E., & Muller, F. (1999). *Language in Time: The Rhythm and Tempo of Spoken Interaction.* Oxford: Oxford University Press.

Bailey, G., Tillery, J., Andres, C. (2005). Some effects of transcribers on data in dialectology. American Speech, 80 (1), 3–21.

Bloom, L. (1993). Transcription and coding for child language research: The parts are more than the whole. In J.A. Edwards & M.D. Lampert (Eds.), *Talking Data: Transcription and Coding in Discourse Research* (pp. 149–166). Mahwah: NJ: Lawrence Erlbaum Associates.

Bucholtz, M. (2000). The politics of transcription. *Journal of Pragmatics*, 32, 1439–1465.

Bucholtz, M. (2007). Variation in transcription. Discourse Studies, 9 (6), 784–808.

Cook, G. (1990). Transcribing infinity: Problems of context presentation. *Journal of Pragmatics*, 14, 1–24.

Coulthard, M. (1996). The official version. Audience manipulation in police records of interviews with suspects. In C.R. Caldas-Coulthard & M. Coulthard (Eds.), *Texts and Practices: Readings in Critical Discourse Analysis* (pp. 166–178). London: Routledge.

Couper-Kuhlen, E. (1993). *English Speech Rhythm: Form and Function in Everyday Verbal Interaction.* Amsterdam: John Benjamins.

Couper-Kuhlen, E. (2000). Prosody. In J. Verschueren, J. Ostman, J. Blommaert & C. Bulcaen (Eds.), *Handbook of Pragmatics* (pp. 1–19). Amsterdam: John Benjamins.

Couper-Kuhlen, E., & Selting, M. (Eds.) (1996). Prosody in Conversation: Interactional Studies. Cambridge: Cambridge University Press

Drahota, A., Costall, A., & Reddy, V. (2008). The vocal communication of different kinds of smile. Speech Communication, 50 (4), 278–287.

Du Bois, J.W. (2006). Transcription delicacy hierarchy. Presented at the *Linguistic Society of America*. Albuquerque, New Mexico.

Du Bois, J.W., Chafe, W.L., Meyer, C., & Thompson, S.A. (2000). *Santa Barbara Corpus of Spoken American English: Part 1.* Philadelphia: Linguistic Data Consortium.

Du Bois, J.W., Schuetze-Coburn, S., Cumming, S., & Paolino, D. (1993). Outline of discourse transcription. In J.A. Edwards & M.D. Lampert (Eds.), *Talking Data: Transcription and Coding in Discourse Research* (pp. 45–89). Mahwah: NJ: Lawrence Erlbaum Associates.

Duranti, A. (2006). Transcripts, like shadows on a wall. Mind, Culture, and Activity, 13 (4), 301–310.

Edwards, D., & Potter, J. (1992). *Discursive Psychology*. London: Sage.

Edwards, J.A., & Lampert, M.D. (Eds.). (1993). *Talking Data: Transcription and Coding in Discourse Research*. Mahwah: Lawrence Erlbaum Associates.

ELAN. Last accessed on 3 January 2011 at: http://www.lat-mpi.eu/tools/elan/

FOLKER. Last accessed on 3 January 2011 at:http://agd.ids-mannheim.de/html/folker_en.shtml

Glenn, P. (2010). Interviewer laughs: Shared laughter and asymmetries in employment interviews. Journal of Pragmatics, 42 (6), 1485–1498.

Goodwin, C. (1980). Restarts, pauses, and the achievement of a state of mutual gaze at turn-beginning. Sociological Inquiry, 50 (3–4), 272–302.

Goodwin, C. (1981). *Conversational Organization: Interaction Between Speakers and Hearers*. New York: Academic Press.

Goodwin, C. (1994). Professional vision. *American Anthropologist*, 96 (3), 606–633.

Goodwin, C. (2000). Action and embodiment within situated human interaction. *Journal of Pragmatics*, 32, 1489–1522.

Goodwin, C. (2003). The body in action. In J. Coupland & R. Gwyn (Eds.), *Discourse, the Body and Identity* (pp. 19–42). New York: Palgrave Macmillan.

Goodwin, M., & Goodwin, C. (2000). Emotion within situated activity. In A. Duranti (Ed.), *Linguistic Anthropology: A Reader* (pp. 239–257). Malden, MA: Blackwell.

Gumperz, J.J., & Berenz, N. (1993). Transcribing conversational exchange. In J.A. Edwards & M.D. Lampert (Eds.), *Talking Data: Transcription and Coding in Discourse Research* (pp. 91–121). Mahwah: NJ: Lawrence Erlbaum Associates.

Hall, J.K. (2007). Readdressing the roles of correction and repair in research on second and foreign language learning. The Modern Language Journal, 91 (4), 511–526.

Hellermann, J. (2003). The interactive work of prosody in the IRF exchange: Teacher repetition in feedback moves. *Language in Society*, 32, 79–104.

Holt, E. (2010). The last laugh: Shared laughter and topic termination. Journal of Pragmatics, 42 (6), 1513–1525.

Hutchby, I., & Wooffitt, R. (2008*). Conversation Analysis*. Cambridge, UK: Polity Press.

Jaffe, A. & Walton, S. (2000). The voices people read: Orthography and the representation of non-standard speech. Journal of Sociolinguistics, 4 (4), 561–587.

Jefferson, G. (1983). Issues in the transcription of naturally-occurring talk: Caricature vs. capturing pronunciational particulars. *Tilburg Papers in Language and Literature*, 34, 1–12.

Jefferson, G. (1985). An exercise in the transcription and analysis of laughter. In T.A. van Dijk (Ed.), *Handbook of Discourse Analysis: Discourse and Dialogue* (pp. 25–34). New York: Academic Press.

Jefferson, G. (2004). Glossary of transcript symbols with an introduction. In G.H. Lerner (Ed.), *Conversation Analysis: Studies from the first generation* (pp. 13–31). Amsterdam: John Benjamins.

Jenks, C.J. (2009). When is it appropriate to talk? Managing overlapping talk in multi-participant voice-based chat rooms. Computer Assisted Language Learning, 22 (1), 19–30.

Keating, E., & Sunakawa, C. (2010). Participation cues: Coordinating activity and collaboration in complex online gaming worlds. *Language in Society*, 39, 331–356.

Kendon, A. (2004). Gesture: Visible Action as Utterance. Cambridge: Cambridge University Press.

Kerswill, P., & Wright, S. (1990). The validity of phonetic transcription: Limitations of a sociolinguistic research tool. *Language Variation and Change*, 2, 255–275.

Krivokapić. J. (2007). Prosodic planning: Effects of phrasal length and complexity on pause duration. *Journal of Phonetics*, 35, 162–179.

Lampert, M.D., & Ervin-Tripp, S.M. (1993). Structured coding for the study of language and social interaction. In J.A. Edwards & M.D. Lampert (Eds.), *Talking Data: Transcription and Coding in Discourse Research* (pp. 169–206). Mahwah: NJ: Lawrence Erlbaum Associates.

Lazaraton, A. (2004). Gesture and speech in the vocabulary explanations of one ESL teacher: A microanalytic inquiry. Language Learning, 54 (1), 79–117.

Levelt, W.J.M. (1983). Monitoring and self-repair in speech. *Cognition*, 14, 41–104.

Ochs, E. (1979). Transcription as theory. In E. Ochs & B. Schieffelin (Eds.), *Developmental Pragmatics* (pp. 43–72). New York: Academic Press.

MacWhinney, B. (1995). *The CHILDES Project: Tools for Analyzing Talk*. Mahwah: NJ: Lawrence Erlbaum Associates.

MacWhinney, B. (2010a). *The CHILDES Project: Tools for Analyzing Talk – Electronic Version. Part 2: The CLAN Programs*. Last accessed on 3 January 2011 at: http://childes.psy.cmu.edu/manuals/clan.pdf

MacWhinney, B. (2010b). *The CHILDES Project: Tools for Analyzing Talk – Electronic Version. Part 1: The CHAT Transcription Format*. Last accessed on 3 January 2011 at: http://childes.psy.cmu.edu/manuals/chat.pdf

Maynard, D. (1991). Interaction and asymmetry in clinical discourse. American Journal of Sociology, 97 (2), 448–495.

Mondada, L. (2007). Commentary: Transcript variations and the indexicality of transcribing practices. Discourse Studies, 9 (6), 809–821.

Mondada, L. (2009). Emergent focused interactions in public spaces: A systematic analysis of the multimodal achievement of a common interactional space. *Journal of Pragmatics*, 41, 1977–1997.

Ofuka, E., McKeown, J.D., Waterman, M.G., & Roach, P.J. (2000). Prosodic cues for rated politeness in Japanese speech. Speech Communication, 32 (3), 199–217.

Pitt, M.A., Johnson, K., Hume, E., Kiesling, S., & Raymond, W. (2005). The Buckeye corpus of conversational speech: Labeling conventions and a test of transcriber reliability. *Speech Communication*, 45, 89–95.

Potter, J., & Hepburn, A. (2010). Putting aspiration into words: 'Laugh particles', managing descriptive trouble and modulating action. Journal of Pragmatics, 42 (6), 1543–1555.

Preston, D.R. (1985). The Li'l Abner syndrome: Written representations of speech. American Speech, 60 (4), 328–336.

Rapley, T. (2007). *Doing Conversation, Discourse and Document Analysis*. London: SAGE Publications.

Roberts, C. (1997). Transcribing talk: issues of representation. TESOL Quarterly, 31 (1), 167–171

Roberts, F., & Robinson, J.D. (2004). Interobserver agreement on first-stage conversation analytic transcription. Human Communication Research, 30 (3), 376–410.

Sacks, H, Schegloff, E.A., & Jefferson, G. (1974). A simplest systematics for the organization of turn-taking for conversation. Language, 50, 696–735.

Schegloff, E.A. (1998). Reflections on studying prosody in talk-in-interaction. *Language and Speech*, 41 (3-4), 235–263.

Schiffrin, D., Tannen, D., & Hamilton, H.E. (Eds.). (2003). The Handbook of Discourse Analysis. Malden, MA: Blackwell.

Schmidt, T. & Schütte, W. (2010). FOLKER: An Annotation Tool for Efficient Transcription of Natural, Multi-party Interaction. In: N. Calzolari (Conference Chair) (Ed.), *Proceedings of the Seventh Conference on International Language Resources and Evaluation* (LREC'10). Valletta, Malta: European Language Resources Association (ELRA)

Selting, M. (1994). Emphatic speech style – with special focus on the prosodic signalling of heightened emotive involvement in conversation. *Journal of Pragmatics*, 22, 375–408.

Selting, M., Auer, P., Barden, B., Bergmann, J., Couper-Kuhlen, E., Gunthner, S., Meier, C., Quasthoff, U., Schlobinski, P., & Uhmann, S. (1998). Gesprachsanalytisches Transkriptionssystem (GAT). *Linguistische Berichte*, 173, 91–122.

Selting, M., Auer, P., Barth-Weingarten, D., Bergmann, J., Bergmann, P., Birkner, K., Couper-Kuhlen, E., Deppermann, A., Gilles, P., Günthner, S., Hartung, M., Kern, F., Mertzlufft, C., Meyer, C., Morek, M., Oberzaucher, F., Peters, J., Quasthoff, U., Schütte, W., Stukenbrock, A., Uhmann, S. (2009). Gesprächsanalytisches Transkriptionssystem 2 (GAT 2). *Gesprächsforschung*, 10, 353–402.

Slobin, D.I. (1993). Coding child language data for crosslinguistic analysis. In J.A. Edwards & M.D. Lampert (Eds.), *Talking Data: Transcription and Coding in Discourse Research* (pp. 207–219). Mahwah: NJ: Lawrence Erlbaum Associates.

Sidnell, J. (2009). Coordinating gesture, talk, and gaze in reenactments. *Research on Language and Social Interaction*, 39 (4), 377–409.

Singer, M., Radinsky, J., & Goldman, S.R. (2008). The role of gesture in meaning construction. *Discourse Processes*, 45, 365–386.

Soanes, C., & Stevenson, A. (Eds.). (2005). *Oxford Dictionary of English* (2nd ed.). Oxford: Oxford University Press.

Sacks, H., Schegloff, E., & Jefferson, G. (1974). A simplest systematics for the organization of turn-taking for conversation. *Language*, 50, 696–735.

Streeck, J. (2008). Gesture in political communication: A case study of the Democratic presidential candidates during the 2004 Primary Campaign. *Research on Language and Social Interaction*, 41 (2), 154–186.

ten Have, P. (2002). Reflections on Transcription. *Cahiers de praxématique*, 39, 21–43.

ten Have, P. (2007). *Doing Conversation Analysis: A Practical Guide*. London: Sage.

Tilley, S.A. (2003). "Challenging" research practices: Turning a critical lens on the work of transcription. Qualitative Inquiry, 9 (5), 750–773.

Transana. Last accessed on 3 January 2011 at:http://www.transana.org/index.htm

Voge, M. (2010). Local identity processes in business meetings displayed through laughter in complaint sequences. Journal of Pragmatics, 42 (6), 1556–1576.

Wade, B., & Moore, M. (1986). Making meaningful choices: An investigation into young children's intonation patterns in storytelling. *Educational Psychology*, 6 (1), 45–56.

Wetherell, M., Taylor, S., & Yates, S. (Eds.). (2001). *Discourse Theory and Practice*. London: Sage.

Wilkinson, R. (2008). Conversation analysis and communication disorders. In M.J. Ball, M.R. Perkins, N. Muller & S. Howard (Eds.), The Handbook of Clinical Linguistics (pp. 92–106). Malden, MA: Blackwell.

Appendices

Appendix A

Example transcript

```
1               (7.2)
2   Peter:      there it is, it's this way
3               ((inaudible))
4               (10.9) ((walking to merchant))
5   Merchant:   hello sir. (0.5) do↓ you↑
6               wa↓nna↑ something?
7               (0.4)
8   Peter:      walk in here and have a look.
9   Merchant:   ((inaudible))
10  Peter:      uh:: maybe. <we::ll see< >we'll
11              see> what we can do
12  Merchant:   o::kay. (.) no problem
13              (0.7)
14  Chris:      you↓ don't↑ remember him?
15              (1.2)
16  Peter:      no:::, we're a[ll
17  Merchant:                 [i remember you
18  Chris:      o:kay=
19  Merchant:   =hehehe
20  Chris:      do you remember he bought=
21  Peter:      =he['s young and hands[ome=
22  Merchant:      [hehe             [no no no
23  Chris:      =he-
24  Peter:      he's young and handsome
25  Chris:      no.
26  Merchant:   no::: >no no>
27  Peter:      and i'm just an ugly old fart
28  Chris:      he ma-
29  Peter:      i know i don't c- [that's okay]
30  Merchant:                     [oh:::::    ]
31              no::: you also (.) NO i remember
32              y[ou
33  Peter:       [don't worry don't worry i
34              don't mind i[f you don't
35  Merchant:               [hehehe
36  Peter:      remember me
```

```
37              (0.6)
38  Merchant:   no I'm j[ust (joke) you
39  Peter:             [i like to be anonymous
40              (1.0) i like to be anonymous
41              okay
42              (1.0)
43  Peter:      it looks like i'll get him that
44              one (3.0) it's too small
45  Merchant:   too small. you↑ want↓ bigger↑
46  Peter:      i think so
47  Merchant:   okay
48  Peter:      i think so
49  Merchant:   yeh smal, i'll choos a large one
50              (4.0)
51  Peter:      uhm (.) (anydeng for * * *) (3.0)
52              he's got a large tee shirt
53              (12.0)
54  Chris:      wht'she lukin for? (.) anarchy?=
55  Merchant:   =(* *)
56              (4.0)
57  Peter:      (* * *) yeah (that's) (* *)
58              (3.0)
59  Peter:      ooops ((bumps into merchandise))
60              (.)
61  Merchant:   that's okay hehehe [sorry
62  Peter:                         [throw
63              everything all over place
64              (1.5)
65  Peter:      °(okay)° can- can↓ we↑ get one
66              [so it's not like] that?
67  Merchant:   [oh >okay. okay.>]
68  Peter:      if you don't mind (1.0)
69              a:nd, what's the price for them
70              (1.0)
71  Merchant:   how much you want?
72              (0.5)
73  Peter:      how much do i want=
74  Merchant:   =ye[s
75  Peter:         [well i- if you're asking, i
76              want you to give it to me=
77  Chris:      =he[he
78  Merchant:      [ha↑hahaha↑ .h[hh
79  Peter:                       [that's i want
80              it for n[othing]
81  Merchant:          [hehehe]
82  Peter:      no money [at all
83  Merchant:           [hehehehe
84  Peter:      no (.) that's not fair (.) so::
85              well it's fair for me but not
```

```
86                  fair for you
87                  (3.0)
88    Peter:        [[so what's your price]]
89    Merchant:     [[i'll give you a good]] price
90    Peter:        because last time you- you sold
91                  it for twenty (yuan)
92    Merchant:     NO::::[::
93    Peter:             [hehe
94    Chris:             [hehe
95    Peter:        you did.
96    Chris:        hehe[hehe
97    Peter:            [(you) (* * *) (1.0) you↑
98                  don't↓ remember↑
99    Merchant:     yeah i don't remember but i know
100                 not twenty
101   Peter:        you su[re?
102   Merchant:           [it was twenty (.) sure
103                 one hundred percent sure
104   Peter:        ha↑hahaha (.) how much was it=
105   Merchant:     =oka[y i'll show you]
106   Peter:            [do you remember] can you
107                 r'mber how much i paid last time
108   Merchant:     last time. (3.5) eight?
109   Peter:        huh?
110   Merchant:     eighty?
111   Peter:        no it wasn't eighty (.) (must) i
112                 ask-ask'm, ok how (m[uch i paid)
113   Merchant:                         [how much?
114   Chris:        tsk[.hhhhhhh
115   Peter:           [i'll tell you what
116                 (1.0)
117   Chris:        i don't remember i thought maybe
118                 (1.0) i thought twenty five
119   Merchant:     ta. hehehe=
120   Chris:        =no?
121   Merchant:     no that's (g[o to)
122   Chris:                    [ehhaha
123   Merchant:     other(hehehe)store (h[elp you)
124   Chris:                             [ehhaha
125   Merchant:     hehehehe.hh
126                 (1.0)
127   Peter:        so (yeah)=
128   Merchant:     =so
129                 (1.5)
130   Peter:        samesize? (1.0) fine. i wonder
131                 it will stay w'n after you wash?
132   Merchant:     no problem
133   Peter:        no problem
134   Merchant:     su[re
```

```
135   Peter:      [you guarantee?
136   Merchant:   yeah i[f this one broken you-]
137   Peter:           [otherwise i would have to
138               come back to china] and bring-=
139   Merchant:   =yes
140   Peter:      and come and see you
141   Merchant:   o[kay
142   Chris:       [ehhaha
143   Peter:      very angry
144   Merchant:   okay
145   Peter:      eh hh[  ha ha  ]
146   Merchant:        [no problem]
147   Peter:      hahaha
148   Merchant:   you stronger th[an me no problem
149   Peter:                     [$°no problem°$
150   Merchant:   yo[u don't a worry]
151   Peter:        [no   no   no ](i know that)
152               okay so we have one at fourty
153   Merchant:   o[kay
154   Peter:       [do i want anything else yeah
155               (1.0) °one at forty° oh sorry
156               [twenty five yeah
157   Chris:      [how much are you paying for it?
158   Peter:      tw[enty five
159   Merchant:     [no::: twenty five
160   Chris:      how much?=
161   Merchant:   =i- i remember not twenty five
162   Peter:      (was it) (1.0) °how much was it°
163               (0.5)
164   Merchant:   fifty
165   Peter:      no it was forty
166   Merchant:   fifty
167   Peter:      it was fo::::rty. yea:::h you
168               know t[hat
169   Merchant:         [okay forty forty forty
170               (1.0)
171   Peter:      eh- right forty it is then
172   Merchant:   okay. so do you need some cap?
173   Peter:      uh:: do i need. (.) no↓ i'm okay
174               thanks=
175   Merchant:   =okay
176   Peter:      i'm okay for a cap
177   Merchant:   okay
178   Peter:      okay so i got forty (.) twenty
179               (.) twenty ((counting money))
180   Chris:      ooh lots of money
181   Peter:      forty (.) lots. lots↑ of↓ money↑
182               lots of money and lots of honey
183               wrapped up in'a five↑pound↓note↑
```

```
184                       (2.0)
185   Merchant:   no problem
186                       (2.0)
187   Peter:      thank you::=
188   Merchant:   =i think maybe you're- you're
189                       big boss so small money for you
190                       people
191   Peter:      i'm not big boss i wish'a- no i
192                       wouldn't want to be big boss
193   Merchant:   °hahaha°
194   Peter:      (°* * * *°) uh no↓ free↑ present
195                       with↓ this↑
196                       (1.0)
197   Merchant:   pre:sent?
198   Peter:      no free present you↑ give↓ me↑
199                       (1.0)
200   Merchant:   no↓::↑
201   Peter:      no no okay eh- eh- r[eally?
202   Merchant:                       [if you
203                       give me fifty i can give you
204                       some (.) small present
205   Peter:      like what? (1.0) if i give you
206                       fifty what will you give me
207                       (.)
208   Merchant:   i'll give you one (* * *)
209                       (1.0)
210   Peter:      one (* * *) hat?
211                       (1.0)
212   Merchant:   no.
213   Peter:      o:h↑ okay↓ i thought you'd give
214                       me da'hat (1.0) yeah [no i don't
215   Merchant:                                [you can
216                       choose      ]
217   Peter:      even want one]
218   Merchant:   or do you want a hat
219   Peter:      no i don't want a hat thanks
220                       it's [okay
221   Merchant:        [you don't want a ha[t?
222   Peter:                                   [thanks
223                       u[hm
224   Merchant:    [something small one?
225   Peter:      uh:no.no i don't need (that one)
226   Merchant:   no? i give free↑ for↓ you↑
227                       (.)
228   Peter:      free?
229   Merchant:   yeah
230   Peter:      you're giving me↑ that↓
231   Merchant:   no. [just'a-        ]
232   Peter:          [that's so kind]
```

```
233   Merchant:   you just'a choose something=
234   Peter:      =no::: no no it's alright=
235   Merchant:   =na↓ha↑[haha i'm sorry]
236   Peter:             [it's okay    ] alright
237               no problem thanks very mu[ch
238   Merchant:                            [okay
239               you're welcome okay have a
((recording stops))
```

Appendix B

Transcription conventions (modified from Atkinson and Heritage, 1984)

[[ ]]	Simultaneous utterances – (beginning [[) and (end]])
[ ]	Overlapping utterances – (beginning [) and (end])
=	Contiguous utterances (or continuation of the same turn)
(0.4)	Represent the tenths of a second between utterances
(.)	Represents a micro-pause (1 tenth of a second or less)
:	Elongation (more colons demonstrate longer stretches of sound)
.	Fall in pitch at the end of an utterance
,	Slight rise in pitch at the end of an utterance
-	An abrupt stop in articulation
?	Rising in pitch at utterance end (not necessarily a question)
CAPTIAL	Loud/forte speech
__	Underline letters/words indicate accentuation
↑↓	Marked upstep/downstep in intonation
° °	Surrounds talk that is quieter
hhh	Exhalations
.hhh	Inhalations
he or ha	Laugh particle
(hhh)	Laughter within a word (can also represent audible aspirations)
> >	Surrounds talk that is spoken faster
< <	Surrounds talk that is spoken slower
(( ))	Analyst notes
( )	Approximations of what is heard
$ $	Surrounds 'smile' voice
*per syllable	Unintelligible syllable

Appendix C

Transcription conventions comparison table

Feature	CA	GAT	SBS
Simultaneous utterances	[[and]]	[and]	[[and]]
Overlapping utterances	[and]	[and]	[1,2,3 and]
Contiguous utterances	=	=	=
Timed pause	(0.0)	(0.0)	(0.0)
Micro pause	(.)	(.)	.. or ...
Falling intonation	.	.	.
Slight rising intonation	,	,	,
Rising intonation	?	?	?.
Marked upstep in intonation	↑	↑	⌉
Marked downstep in intonation	↓	↓	⌋
Elongation	:	:	:
Abrupt stop	-	-	-
Emphasis	underline	CAPITAL	^
Loud/forte speech	CAPITAL	<<f>word>	<F>word</F>
Soft/piano speech	° °	<<p>word>	<P>word</P>
Exhalations	hhh	hhh°	(Hx)
Laugh particle	he or ha	he or ha	@
Laughter within a word	wo(hh)rd	<<laugh>word>	wo@rd
Inhalations	.hhh	°hhh	(H)
Faster/allegro talk	>word<	<<all>word>	
Slower/lento talk	<word>	<<len>word>	
Smile voice	$word$	<<:-)>word>	<☺>word</☺>
Analyst notes	((notes))	((notes))	((notes))
Unintelligible syllable	*per syllable	x per syllable	# per syllable
Hearing approximations	(word)	(word)	#word

Appendix D

Quick start guide to transcribing

Before beginning (and during) the transcription process, it is important to keep in mind the main reason for transcribing communication data. Transcripts of communication data are created for the purpose of carrying out research on talk and interaction. They are analytic tools that help researchers make sense of the primary source of data: audio/video recordings. During the entire transcription process, a researcher must establish and maintain an understanding of how a transcript will be used for analytic purposes, as research traditions and aims will inform the decisions made during the various transcription steps identified below.

Put differently, a researcher must not begin the transcription process without knowing why a transcript is needed in the first place. Is a transcript that includes prosodic features needed to conduct research, or will a less detailed, orthographic transcript provide the necessary information? These are only two of the many issues that are potentially relevant to formulating a plan for transcribing communication data. Accordingly, the steps identified below should not, in any way, replace a thorough reading of this book. It is also important to note that some researchers may approach the task of transcribing in a slightly different order than the steps identified below.

So, what does transcription work entail after data collection?

1. Back up data recordings: no data, no transcripts!
2. Create a file-naming system (see Section 3.3.1).
3. Create log files, which document any relevant information that is not immediately available/included in the transcript (e.g., recording dates and contextual information).
4. Create pseudonyms for people and place names, if necessary (see Section 2.5). This information can be stored in the log files.
5. Determine what software program(s) will be used to play back and transcribe data recordings (see Sections 3.2 and 6.3.6). Using transcription software will make **Step 7** and **Step 8** redundant.
6. Determine what level of detail (granularity) is initially needed (see Section 3.4.3). This will be closely related to research traditions and aims (see Section 2.2).
7. Determine the layout of the transcript (see Section 3.3).
8. Determine how lines will be numbered (see Section 3.3.2).
9. Select a transcription system for interactional and paralinguistic features (see Chapter 4).

10. Begin transcribing data recordings (see Chapter 3).
10a. Two common approaches exist for **Step 10**: (1) transcribe orthographic detail first, and then interactional and prosodic detail, or (2) transcribe orthographic and interactional and prosodic detail at the same time (see Section 3.4.3).
10b. In addition to transcribing data recordings according to a predetermined level of granularity, researchers must decide how the orthographic detail will be transcribed. Will vernacularization or standardization be used (see Sections 2.4, 6.3.1, and 6.3.2)?
10c. Review the empirical literature that will be used to conduct the research. This will help researchers make any necessary adjustments to the level of granularity needed (see Section 2.2).
10d. Share various versions of the transcript with work colleagues. The aim is to clarify difficult-to-hear words and utterances, fine-tune other aspects of the transcript, and refine the analytic observations made with the transcript (see Section 6.2.2).
10e. Back up the transcript.
10f. Repeat Steps **10c-10f** until research objectives are met.

Index

A
accent x, 61
accentuation 55, 60–61, 114
actions 7, 48, 74, 77
alignment 40, 102
amplitude 43, 55, 60, 71
anonymity 6, 23, 82–84
apostrophes 97–98
approximations 18, 42, 52, 68–69, 114–115
arrows 3, 38, 58, 66, 86
Audacity 102
auto-numbering 34–35

B
brackets 31, 40, 48–50, 61–62
breathing 63, 65
Bucholtz 4–5, 9, 17–20, 29

C
capital 61–62, 64–65, 96–97, 115
carriage return 35–36
CHAT 46, 102
CHILDES 102
columns 30–31, 99
compatibility 100, 103
computer-assisted 62, 101–102
contextual 2, 4, 27, 39, 116
contiguous 48–49, 51–52, 114–115
conventions 26, 45–49, 71, 78, 96–98, 100, 114–115
conversation analysis x, 1, 12–13, 16, 22, 46

D
data analysis 11–14, 15, 32, 104
database 102–103
data session 93
data workshop 92
detail 3, 5, 8–9, 12–13, 25, 39, 42–43, 55, 82–84, 95, 116–117
digital 23, 78–79, 82–83
downstep 58, 114–115

Du Bois 42, 46–47
Duranti 4, 11, 14–15, 17, 91

E
ELAN 101
elongation 43, 55, 59–60, 66, 114–115
emphasis 60–61, 115
enter key (see carriage return)
ethics 21–22, 42
exhalations 63–65, 114–115
eye dialect 19–20

F
faster 66, 114–115
floor 53, 59–60, 95, 98–99
FOLKER 101–102
full stop 3, 54, 56–57, 65

G
gaze 1, 4–5, 52, 71–72, 74–77, 80, 86
Gesprächsanalytisches Transkriptionssystem 46
GAT 46–48, 53–54, 56, 58–69, 115
gesture 73, 76–77, 82–83, 85–88
Goodwin 16, 52, 55, 71–73, 76–78
granularity 43, 45, 55, 80, 82, 116–117
graphics editor 72, 81–82

H
hardware x, 25, 28–29
hearing 68–69, 91–92

I
identity 22–24, 83–84
inhalation 63, 65, 114–115
interactional x, 1–2, 4–5, 20, 31, 42–43, 45–48, 53–54, 59, 61, 63, 71–74, 78, 94–95, 100, 102, 116–117

International Phonetic Alphabet 4, 19–21
involvement x, 15, 89–90, 92–94

J
Jefferson 15, 19, 46, 48, 63

K
Kendon 72, 74

L
latching 51–52
laughter 15, 63–65, 67, 114–115
layout 7, 25–26, 29, 30, 32–33, 37, 98, 116
levels 43
line breaks 25, 35–38
line numbers 25, 30–31, 34–35, 37–38, 82, 101–102
log files 116
loud 60–62, 114–115

M
MacWhinney 46, 102
margins 30–32, 36
media 24, 26–27, 52, 72–73, 75, 77–80, 84–87, 91, 101–102
medium 2, 4–5, 7, 9, 15, 73, 82
methodology 9, 11–15, 42
Mondada 17, 71, 76, 104
movement 72, 78, 85–87

N
nonverbal behavior 71–72, 75, 78
nonverbal conduct x, 71–88, 102
numbering 34–36, 51, 86

O
Ochs 4, 11, 29
organization 25, 29, 75
orthographic 19, 26, 43, 95, 116–117
outsourcing 90, 94–95

overlapping 31, 40–41, 47–52, 114–115

P
paralinguistic 40–41, 43, 45–47, 54–55, 67–68, 100, 116
parentheses 53–54, 64–65, 68–69, 79
particle 63–65, 114–115
pause 34, 38, 48, 53–54, 114–115
period (see full stop)
pitch 15, 56–57, 114
placement 4, 25, 39, 53, 60
playback 24–25, 26–29, 52, 91
political 11, 18, 21, 98
portability 30–32, 35–36, 38–39, 100
positions 57–59, 71–78, 80, 82, 85–88
pronunciation particulars 21
prosody 47, 54, 56
proximity 71, 74, 77
pseudonym 23
punctuation 3, 46–47, 56, 57, 96

Q
quality 4, 6, 28, 45, 52, 67, 103
question mark 57–58

R
readability 29, 30, 32, 36, 38–40, 49–51, 55, 57, 79–80, 95–97, 100

referencing 33
research traditions 3, 9, 32, 43, 78, 116
rows 32, 35–38, 40

S
Santa Barbara School 46
SBS 46–48, 51, 53–54, 56–57, 59, 61–69, 115
selection 41, 94
Selting 46–47, 60, 66, 71
semiotic 73, 76–77
sequence x, 33, 35, 86, 88
simultaneous 48–49, 98, 114–115
slower 66–67, 114–115
smile 67, 75, 114–115
soft 60, 62–63, 115
software 8, 16, 22, 25–29, 52, 56, 58–59, 72–73, 80, 82, 85, 87–88, 91–92, 100–101, 103, 116
spacing 25, 37–38, 40
speaker 25, 30–32, 41
specialist 82, 85, 90–91, 94
speech community 20–21
spelling 19–21
standardization 19–21, 103, 117
still images 80
stops 54–55, 59–60, 114–115
stress 22–23, 43, 45, 54–55, 60
subjectivity 11
syllable 23, 58, 68–69, 115
symbols 3, 40–41, 45–49, 55–60, 62, 67, 85–87, 95, 100

T
tabulation 38
temporality 84–88
tempo 55, 66
terminal 48–49, 51
theory 12
time stamps 33, 85–88, 102
timing 26, 52
Transana 102
translation 99–100
turn transitions 32, 50, 53, 60

U
underline 61, 114–115
unicode 41
unintelligible 55, 68, 115
upstep 57–58, 114–115
utterance 30–32, 37, 49–51, 56–58, 61–65, 88, 96

V
variation 4, 9, 14–18, 23, 100, 103
vernacularization 19–21, 117

W
white space 36–38, 50
word processing programs 8, 35, 39, 101–103
written conventions 96–97